Morley Roberts

Land-Travel and Sea-Faring

Morley Roberts

Land-Travel and Sea-Faring

ISBN/EAN: 9783337206215

Printed in Europe, USA, Canada, Australia, Japan

Cover: Foto ©Andreas Hilbeck / pixelio.de

More available books at **www.hansebooks.com**

LAND-TRAVEL AND SEA-FARING

LAND-TRAVEL

AND

SEA-FARING

BY
MORLEY ROBERTS
AUTHOR OF "THE WESTERN AVERNUS," ETC

ILLUSTRATED BY A. D. McCORMICK

London
LAWRENCE AND BULLEN
169 NEW BOND STREET, W.
1891

RICHARD CLAY AND SONS, LIMITED,
LONDON AND BUNGAY.

PREFATORY NOTE.

MUCH of the material in this book has been previously published, and I have to thank the Editors of the *Cornhill*, *Murray's Magazine*, and the *Field*, for their kind permission to reprint what appeared in their pages.

MORLEY ROBERTS.

October 28th, 1891.

CONTENTS.

CHAPTER I.
A STEERAGE PASSAGE . . . . PAGE 1

CHAPTER II.
IN MELBOURNE CITY 32

CHAPTER III.
ON THE BANKS OF THE MURRAY 49

CHAPTER IV.
AT DORA DORA 59

CHAPTER V.
THROUGH THE BULL PLAINS 85

CHAPTER VI.
THE GREAT HEAT 108

CHAPTER VII.
CARABOBLA AND YARRA YARRA 118

CONTENTS.

CHAPTER VIII.
A THREE MONTHS' RIDE 132

CHAPTER IX.
BURRAWANG 154

CHAPTER X.
TOWARDS THE WILLANDRA 167

CHAPTER XI.
THE LAND OF SHEEP 181

CHAPTER XII.
HUNGER AT BULLIGAL CREEKS 214

CHAPTER XIII.
IN THE FOC'SLE 230

LAND-TRAVEL AND SEA-FARING.

CHAPTER I.

A STEERAGE PASSAGE.

IT was on a miserably dull and sunless day, in that Liverpool which never looks to me more than barely cheerful even in fine weather, that I went on board the *Seringapatam*, lying in the Albert Dock, as a steerage passenger to Melbourne. It was my first flight into the outer world of which I have since then seen so much, and being not yet nineteen and tolerably inexperienced, the contrast between what I had known, and the first aspect of what I was to know too well, was very grievous to me. In spite of the fearful joys of that freedom for which I had longed, I was almost ready to return to my North-country home, though I would have died sooner than confess it even to myself.

The quarters to be occupied by the steerage passengers, who numbered about twenty, were in the 'tween-decks abaft the mainmast, and when I saw that "steerage" might be adequately paraphrased only by "Black Hole," I was sorry that I had saved a portion of my money by adopting the cheapest method of crossing half the world. I had never suspected that I was to lie cheek by jowl, four in a bunk, with unclean Irish emigrants of unsavoury aspect and odour, nor that the flourishing list of provisions named on the Passage Ticket meant uneatable food and semi-starvation for one hundred and two days of an unlucky, remarkable, and extremely slow voyage.

Of the twenty men, women, and children who were to be my companions for that long time, the men were either helplessly drunk, or halfway at least to that seemingly desired end, some being irritatingly hilarious, some viciously quarrelsome, and others maudlin and tearful. The deck beneath one's feet in the narrow dark steerage was filthy, and an oil-lamp of vile smell, hung overhead on a wire hook, added most unnecessarily to the sickening odour of mixed humanity, while drops of condensed foul breath dropped from the deck above upon the unclean tables, encumbered with bundles of clothes and bursting portmanteaus which had last rested in mud and slush on the damp wharves. The women, who were for the most part unmistakably Irish, sat in this den of discomfort either weeping and disconsolate, or else quarrelling feebly with their dirty brats of children, who wailed or screamed for ever without cessation; while some few ate bread and strong cheese, which contended, not wholly in vain, with rival smells, and drank stale beer out of long-necked spirit-bottles. It was among such surroundings, with such companions, that I was to pass nearly four months of my life, and though I have suffered, toiled and starved in many parts of the world since then, nothing that I have seen or gone through can ever efface the effect that the 'tween-decks of the *Seringapatam* had upon me, when I crawled doubtfully down the companion-ladder to survey my temporary home.

Next to us of the steerage, and only divided from it by a few rough boards and a doorway without a door, was the second-class berth, in which I could see three or four young men, more of my own class, sitting in melancholy mood, as though they considered their lot little better than our own, in spite of the higher fare they had paid. As it was among these men that I usually lived, in spite of my being a steerage passenger, I will devote a few words to their description, histories, and character, which will show that I had certainly come to a bright school to learn rascality.

The first in my mind is a man named Broome, whom I got to know extremely well before I reached Australia, and with whom I lived for many months in that country. He was about twenty-seven, tall and very thin, but with broad shoulders as square as the angle between a cow's tail and her straight spine; his eyes were a beautiful bright blue, and on his pale cheeks blazed two spots of hectic colour. He looked as if he were dying, but he was, as a matter of fact, just recovering from a long and severe illness. Whether he had been sent on this voyage for the sake of his health, or, as he said, because he had made his native town too hot to hold him, I cannot say; but if his appearance suggested the one, his uncommon recklessness, which, apparent at first, increased immensely as he improved in health, made the other at least as likely. But Broome was a gentleman by manners and education, and as such, stood a head and shoulders above his berth-mates.

Next to him I remember an unmistakable English cad, just one remove from an 'Arry, who always said he was *Mr.* Jackson, if asked his name. He had small nondescript-coloured eyes, no complexion, large hands and feet, a vile London accent, and to add to those original sins, he wore serge clothes of the colour affected by low Italians round Saffron

Hill. I could pardon the effrontery with which he told us that he was obliged to leave England because he had embezzled money from his employer in order to take a trip to France, but I could never forgive the hue of his garments.

A tall, fine-looking man of about thirty, named Cotton, was with us, because he had, in his capacity as agent for a Manchester house, ordered a quantity of linen goods which he had sold for his own benefit. It was due to the exertions of his family that he had only been punished by exile, and not imprisonment.

There was also a consumptive pawnbroker's assistant, named Beaumont, and Harry Salton, a Yorkshireman, and a fine healthy specimen of a country-bred Englishman. Beaumont was considered a criminal, and humorously called a "fence," on account of his trade; but Salton had done nothing disgraceful, as far as could be learnt, which was a sort of distinction in the second cabin, where the only other man I have not named, Harrison, was sent out of the country because, having persistently refused to earn a living for himself, he had managed to exist in a more disgraceful manner. If I never quite succeeded in fitting myself for companionship on equal terms with such as my new acquaintances, it is probably owing to a natural obstinacy which inclines me to go my own way towards good or towards evil; but if I had showed a little more plasticity and pliability of character, I might have graduated as a first-class scoundrel in the shortest time on record, considering the able coaches around me on all sides.

Our ship was still lying in the dock, where she was to remain till early morning, while I was in the company of these young men, and when I got sick both of them and the tainted atmosphere, I went ashore to prowl round curiously in the lowest parts of Back Goree, where the worst slums of Liverpool are situated. The villainous faces of crimps and loafers passed me as I hurried on, taking instinctive care not to loiter or look about too much. Since that day I have rambled in the evilest parts of many great cities, and have rarely been molested so long as I put on the air of having business in that quarter, and looked as if I were going somewhere in particular. Yet I wonder I did not fall a victim to my rashness and undimmed natural verdure, when I ventured, having much money on me, into dens and drinking places that I should now never think of entering unless in company with a policeman or detective. But I was drawn on and fascinated by the rampant disorder that I saw round me. I passed down back alleys and courts, and dimly-lighted slums, and standing in foul doorways to let some hideous nocturnal procession pass, I heard fouler language, and saw things and faces that made my flesh crawl with horror. I heard fights and oaths, and dreadful yells, and sometimes the sound of broken glass and crockery as a jug came through a dirt-grimed window and struck the opposing obscene wall. When at last I went on board ship, it was with a feeling of relief and escape, and as I stumbled down the awkward ladder into the reeking atmosphere of the 'tween-decks, I was thankful even for that refuge from the human animals beyond the high dock walls. Yes, even though my three bunk companions were half intoxicated and loathsome. By the dawn of day we were at sea, behind a tug that steamed against half a gale from the south-west.

Of our whole crew, only the captain, the two mates and four apprentices were English, and the remainder a queer motley conglomeration of Hindoos, Malays, and Kroomen from Africa, who outnumbered the white men, even when all the passengers were counted in. For the *Seringapatam* was a large full-rigged ship of more than 1,600 tons register, and carried forty-five Lascars, where some eighteen Englishmen would have been deemed amply sufficient. We had all types of countenances on board, from the finely-cut faces of some higher-caste Hindoos to those possessed by poor inferior fellows with whom they would not eat; to the semi-Papuan physiognomy of the Malays, and the negrine character of the big-limbed Krooman. The serang, or bo'son, of this various-coloured Calashee crowd was a Malay of a short stout figure, with a scant bristly brush of a moustache, and twinkling black eyes, who soon got to know me so well, that I often heard him demanding "Where Robert, where Robert?" if he wanted me to help him in deciphering the tallies of the sails in the sail locker, when his want of knowledge of writing and the impatience of the others left him helpless and bewildered among a pile of pieces of wood which he was to attach to the sails they named. The chief steward was a Hindoo, with the most delicate clearly-cut features I ever saw on a man, while his complexion was comparatively light. Although very small-boned and slender, he was strangely powerful for his build, and could do tricks of strength with his lady-like wrist and fingers which puzzled even the biggest among us, and I dare say even the Krooman, Tom, who was a negro Hercules, might have found him no mean opponent.

I had plenty of opportunity for observation, for I was not, indeed I never have been, sea-sick in the least; so while most of my new acquaintances were groaning over their misdeeds in the truest repentance they were ever likely to feel, I was able to keep the decks with Broome, who, having been a sailor for some years, was unaffected by the heavy sea into which we dived close-hauled. For a fortnight we had one breeze after another, and "breeze" in the sailor's sense of the word means something extremely like a storm, for leaving England in the last week in September, we got all the cream of the equinoctial gales, enjoying at last in the Bay of Biscay a real "snorter" for three days, during which we were hove to under the lower maintopsail. It was the first storm I had ever seen at sea, and I so thoroughly delighted in it, that no sooner did I get drenched through on deck, than I went below to change my clothes only in order that I might come up to be again soused in the lee scuppers. The *Seringapatam* was a very "wet ship," that is, she was very much inclined to ship heavy seas, so when she rolled to windward every now and again, one came on board and filled the main deck, while the water poured over the fok'sle head like a cataract; and if it took away the scuttle there, as it sometimes did, the water rushed through the men's quarters like a mill stream. But my chief interest was naturally in the unfortunate steerage, and not there.

When this gale had been blowing tremendously hard for twenty-four hours, it blew much harder for another twenty-four, and finally exhausted its energy in a terrific burst, which did not then in the least alarm me, as I was almost ignorant that it really was a "living gale." But if I thought little of it, the Irish men and women did not, and believed their last hour was come, as they sat or kneeled, praying, howling, screaming and wailing loud or low in the intervals of sea-sickness, while the water washed about on the dirty decks, and the chests, breaking their lashings, threatened to brain those who attempted to control their career. The hatch above was kept closed, and by night and day the oil-lamp swung to and fro, or round and round, dimly illuminating our den, the atmosphere of which became closer and fouler yet than it was at the best of times, while each roll or heavy pitch of the labouring vessel was greeted with heartrending howls of anguish, or groans of despair. The only time I saw these folks take the least interest in what any one else did or said was when I incurred the wrath of two of the women. As I was coming down below, and was just about to shut the door of the booby-hatch, the vessel gave a very heavy lee roll; the lashings of the ladder parted, leaving me swinging in the air, until a sea came over the weather rail, and rushing down to leeward, shut the door on the finger-nails of my right hand. I let go, and on reaching the deck I swore, very naturally as I think under the circumstances, considering that I was also wetted to the skin by the water which came in on top of me; but my excited language roused the fiercest wrath of these two devout Catholics, who screamed with horror at me and vowed I should sink the ship. In calm weather they did not mind far worse language in the least, and their husbands and brothers swore on in sunshine unreproved; but now I had to retreat from them into the second cabin and wait until they calmed down, which they did not wholly do until it was evident that the vessel was not sinking, and that the gale was blowing itself out.

I was soon on very bad terms with some of the men in the steerage, whose ways were naturally very displeasing to me, for my ideas of refinement had not been acquired in a mud cabin along with a pig. I dare say I was a little bumptious too, which perhaps irritated them, but at any rate I was almost always on the verge of a row with one or the other of them. Hence I was naturally driven into the second cabin, where men were whose notions of cleanliness were more on a par with my own, or into

the company of the Lascars, who were always civil and kind to me. I have sat for many hours in their quarters, which did not smell as bad as my own, even if there were some strange odours with which I was unacquainted, talking and making signs to a Malay or Hindoo, even making friends of one of the big Kroomen, who, though possessed of the finest physique on board, was lower in intelligence than the lowest of the others. A few of them understood some English, and I gradually picked up a little Hindostanee and a few Malay phrases; but my chief Oriental chum was a bright-eyed, lithe-limbed lad from the French Indian Settlement, who always went by the name of Pondicherry. He could talk a sort of French very fluently, and as I had some knowledge of that language, he would interpret for or to me. I think I have been in few stranger places than that fok'sle at night with the dim light vaguely illuminating the swarthy faces and the flashing eyes of that mixed Oriental crew, as they sat round me smoking and talking garrulously in a strange Babel of tongues and dialects, while my own figure and comparatively fair complexion added, I dare say, to the interest of the scene in a way I could not then comprehend, but which now requires little imagination to conceive.

Pondicherry never got to understand how it was I knew French, and often tried to make me explain; but my attempts simply added to his bewilderment. My own impression is that he thought French was a language only spoken at his native place, for he was always trying to inveigle me into an acknowledgment that I had been there, and when I denied it, he shook his head mysteriously.

These men often offered me something to eat, which, when it was not shark ten days old, I was often glad enough to accept, for the steerage fare was as insufficient in quantity as it was vile in quality; indeed, if it had not been occasionally supplemented by the good-will of the Hindoo cooks, or men, and a fair supply of hard biscuit, which was the only thing I found always eatable, I might have gone as hungry on board ship as I have since been on the tramp in Australia or America.

We had been forty-seven days out from Liverpool when we at last drifted over the line, for after the final gale in the Bay of Biscay, we had experienced nothing but light or contrary winds, and the north-east trades were just at that season conspicuous by their absence. Or if they blew, it was only faintly. But when we caught the south east trades, they, as if to make up for the shortcomings of the northern winds, blew almost tempestuously, and we ran through their latitudes under shortened canvas. When we commenced to run our easting down and get to the southward of the Cape, we began to have a lively time. It is only a popular superstition that Cape Horn is the most tempestuous place in the world, for although it knows how to blow there and to blow tremendously hard, the sea, even when it runs high, is always comparatively regular. The Cape of Good Hope, or "the Cape" *par excellence*, has, however, a broken choppy sea, owing to the various currents meeting there, and the variability of the winds, which makes it a far more dangerous place than its more feared and colder brother promontory at the south of America. Yet the cold to the southward of the

Cape was severe enough as we rounded it, and some of the Lascars, who feel such weather extremely, hid themselves and refused to go aloft. They were like the sergeant of the Black West Indian Regiment who remarked to his officer that "it was too cold for brave to-day," and some of those who were smart and active when it was warm, were the worse skulkers when the weather changed for the worse. For though they clothed themselves with every garment they possessed, until there was a small quantity of Lascar to a large quantity of clothing, they still shivered in a most extraordinary manner. I remember it had been blowing hard all one day from the south-west in heavy squalls, with some sleet mingled with cold rain, and on going on deck late in the evening I saw Mahomet, a rather good-looking Hindoo, who had once offered me some ancient shark which fairly took my breath away, standing under the break of the poop looking so cold and miserable that I thought, in spite of his unaccustomed bulk, he was insufficiently clothed. I asked him if it was so, and I found he had on two coats, two waistcoats, and *seven* shirts, while over all he wore his oilskins.

My friend Tom, the big Krooman, turned sulky and refused to do any work, although exercise would have kept him from being blue with cold. The mate, Mr. Mackintosh, a regular old sea-dog, who had been seventeen years before the mast before he thought of getting a second officer's certificate, had the man handcuffed and brought aft on the poop. And poor Tom's endurance, if foolish, was really splendid. He lay on the wheel-gratings without shelter, and with no more clothing than shirt and trousers, for four whole days, during which it sometimes snowed and oftener rained; nor would the officers allow him more covering lest he might elect

to stay there if he were made too comfortable. He had nothing given him to eat but biscuits, and he drank only water; but still he would not return to work. On the third day the captain, who was by no means a brutal man, offered to release him if he would only condescend to go into the sail locker and make sinnet (a kind of plait made of rope yarns). I was standing near, pitying the poor devil, and hoped he would take the offer. But no; Tom shook his head, he would do nothing. At last, in the evening of the fourth day he caved in, for the night looked as if it would be bitterly cold, and he was assisted forward to his bunk, where some hot coffee was given him. It had been pitiful to see that huge black Hercules, lying there curled up in an animal-like bunch, with his skin turned a sort of dull blue, shivering violently, but as firm and obstinate as adamant in making a martyr of himself, although it was difficult to see what other course could be taken with him, considering that if he had beaten the officers, the others, who were only too ready to skulk, would have imitated his example. Yet I used to wonder what thoughts were passing through his thick skull when I was on the poop at night and saw him there, for when I said to him quietly, " Tom, go to work and don't be a fool," he only looked at me dully, shrugged his tremendous shoulders, and shivered until I gave him a piece of tobacco. But he bore no malice to the officers for what they had done, and when the weather became warmer he was as fine and willing a worker as any on the ship.

The Lascars behaved very differently from Tom, and not having the courage to absolutely refuse to do anything, they tried malingering or shamming. Sometimes they deceived the captain; but more often the sight of the dreadful dose of castor-oil, which was his universal remedy in suspected cases, restored them to sudden health and vigour. It was only the very determined ones who had the courage to swallow the nauseous dose, even although they were ensured a few idle hours by taking it.

Few incidents of importance occurred from the time we were well to the eastward of the Cape, until we were south of Cape Leeuwin, the most westerly point of the great Australian Bight, beyond a few rows among us in the steerage, which was becoming, for unspeakable reasons, almost uninhabitable by a person of any cleanliness, and the broaching of the cargo by the second-class passengers, who, by drawing some nails with great skill, managed to steal several cases of the finest Irish whiskey.

Strange as it may seem from what occurred off the Leeuwin, our captain was a total abstainer. But to make up for this sobriety, his wife, a fine handsome woman she was, invariably took too much to drink when it blew heavily, and increased her doses in proportion to the violence of the storm. Thus she was, as we often remarked, a registering barometer, that did not foretell heavy weather, but only recorded it, and her being moderately excited with liquor indicated that it was blowing a stiff breeze, while her wild appearance and staggering gait were sufficient, without any other evidence of the senses, to show that we were under storm canvas. But never until the gale off the Leeuwin did she entirely lose control over herself and finally become insensible, which shows that the weather there surpassed in violence anything we had experienced in the Bay or off the Cape of Good Hope. And indeed this was so.

It had been Mr. Mackintosh's middle watch that night, and not liking the look of the weather, he took in some of the lighter canvas just before he went below at four o'clock. The second mate, Mr. Ladd, although the weather grew worse yet, did not shorten sail further, and when the captain came on deck he ordered those sails to be set which Mackintosh had stowed four hours previously. The second officer stared a little when he received his superior's orders, but of course said nothing, although the wind was now coming in heavy puffs from the west, and the sea was rising rapidly. By this time, from my own experience and from the face of Ladd, I could see we were probably in for a heavy gale, and boy-like, I was pleased at the prospect. For within certain limits a storm at sea always exhilarates me in a most marked degree, and I am never so merry as when it blows hard. This, too, promised to be a sight worth seeing, for there was no sign of rain, and the sky was not quite overclouded until noon, by which time the wind was reaching its maximum. During the first few hours the sun shone brightly through the drifting clouds; the waves rose higher and higher, yet in great blue masses tipped with foam that suddenly dropped, as if their foundations had been instantly rent away, to leave great hollows and swirls coloured light blue and green where the foam-bubbles and driven air mingled with the purer blue; while down the leeward side of the vast valleys ran thin ribands of white, and to windward the gale drew, as it were, a brush across the lifted wall, marking it with bands, notching it here and there, and at the summit turning it to pure white and foam-smoke, that streamed out on the level wind.

At eight o'clock Mr. Mackintosh came on deck again, and as he stood near me I could see he was angry at the conduct of the captain. I suppose Ladd told him what had happened, for he only greeted his superior officer with a rather surly "good morning," and made no remark to him. With the skipper on deck taking an interest in matters, it was no part of his duty to shorten sail, and within a quarter of an hour it was beyond any one's power to again furl the sails he had taken in at first, for the skysail and three royals suddenly disappeared, leaving only a few fragments attached to the yards. Every one who was on deck expected to hear the order to shorten sail, but our unmoved skipper hardly took notice of what was happening, and walked up and down the poop, smoking his pipe in the most undisturbed manner. I am almost afraid that sailors will not believe that any one in command of a big vessel could act as he did, but I am ready to vouch for the truth of every word I set down here, and can even bring corroborative evidence. For not one sail did the captain order to be stowed save the mainsail, which was driving her almost under the water. That was taken in with infinite labour at ten o'clock, but though the force of the wind momentarily increased until it blew a hurricane, he never even tried to reef the topsails before they went. Before that, the three topgallant sails vanished one by one, and then two of the three upper topsails were blown out of their bolt-ropes with a report like thunder, and inside of half an hour the mizen and main lower topsails followed suit. Then the cro'jack sheets parted, and the cro'jack flogging the yard in ribbons. The only sail we saved in fair condition was the upper main topsail, and that the two mates, the Serang, two quarter-masters, Broome, Salton and myself took in. For by this time I was quite accustomed to go aloft, and we volunteered because most of the Lascars and Malays were fairly frightened and would not leave the deck. They stowed themselves away in every hole and corner they could find, and out of forty-five there were only three in the topsail yard with us.

I have said it was blowing a hurricane, and I mean what I say. Since then I have seen it blow hard, and I had known some bad weather, as I have said, in the Bay and off the Cape; but this fairly came out ahead of anything I have ever known for violence, though it scarcely rained during the whole thirty-six hours it lasted, and still remained warm. The torn and driven sea, under the rainless canopy of low drifting clouds, was cruel and ghastly to look at, and the waves were as big as the rollers off the Horn. When I went up aloft I had nothing on but an old cap, a cotton shirt and a pair of old trousers; but when I came down I was minus the shirt, for it had been ripped into pieces which struck me about the face, until I had assisted the wind with my hands and got rid of it, and my cap, which blew off and went so far that I did not see it drop. We were up aloft for two hours, and though the sea ran heavier and heavier, and the rolling and pitching of the vessel increased more and more, I dare to say that I still found it very interesting. As we tugged at the bellying sail that stretched out in front of us as stiff as a board, I found time at intervals to cast a look down upon the raging gulf below, and the narrow wet deck which was sometimes beneath us and then suddenly to our right or left. As we pitched, the water came in over the bows and poured in a white and green cataract over the fok'sle head; as we rolled, it came in great masses over the rail, until it filled up the main deck and escaped through the stove-in main deck ports and scupper holes. Sometimes the following sea even overtook and pooped us, that is, came in over the stern, and poured down on the main deck. It was fortunate for us that we did not injure or lose our rudder, for if we had come broadside on to the wind, it would have been good-bye for all of us. When we had the topsail stowed in some sort of a fashion we went down and got some whiskey, for, strange to say, our teetotal captain let us have as much as we wanted. And some of us appeared to want a great deal, for about three o'clock, Mackintosh, Ladd, Salton and Broome were all very drunk indeed. It may appear invidious of me to claim the distinction of being the only tolerably sober man among those who did any work, but as a matter of fact this was so, for even the apprentices were "half-seas over."

Shortly after four o'clock I quitted the deck for a little while to put on another coat, and came up again in less than five minutes to see Mr. Ladd sitting in the main hatch, smothered in blood. I ran to him in great alarm and asked what the matter was. He emitted a tremendous volley of oaths, and ended by roaring, "Mutiny! mutiny!" I left him and went forward. Just by the cook's galley I met Mr. Mackintosh, in a worse plight, if possible, than the second officer, for the blood was streaming from a cut in his head, one eye was quite closed up, and the rest of his face was hardly to be distinguished. He too was swearing, and, holding on to the deckhouse, he likewise roared "Mutiny!" I caught his arm, guided him to the main hatch, where a sea presently washed over them, and ran to meet Salton and Broome, who were coming forward, telling them what I had gathered vaguely, that the

mates had gone into the fok'sle to turn the men out to work and had got severely thrashed for their pains. We all looked at each other and at the Lascars, who were standing in a crowd at the port door of the fok'sle armed with handspikes and belaying-pins, and without further enquiry Broome rushed into the cook's galley on one side, seized a long carving-knife, and emerged from the other uttering a howl like a fiend's. Salton produced a sixshooter, and I, not to be behind-hand, grabbed an iron belaying-pin. I had no distinct notion of what we were to do, but I followed Broome, who sprang into the fok'sle at a bound. There were some forty men inside, and we were three; but I verily believe Broome would have charged an army at that moment, and our audacity carried the day. To say the Lascars ran like sheep would be to put it mildly; for they yelled with terror, and fled like smoke before the wind. In half a minute they were crowded on the deck outside. Broome was threatening to have the life of any one who murmured, and Salton made first one and then the other cower and shrink by pointing his sixshooter at him. I came near getting my skull cracked, and was hit slightly on the shoulder. But when I was in the open again I recovered some slight degree of common sense, and rushed off for the captain. Surely the man was the strangest mixture of courage and cowardice I ever saw, for though he was white and almost trembling, he came forward without a weapon. We were both knocked down by a sea close to the main hatch, where the mates were still sitting, but when we picked ourselves up, we went towards the crew. The captain ordered them into the fok'sle again, and they went like lambs, for Salton joined in with his weapon. Then he commanded Broome to put down his knife. No, he would do nothing of the sort, but danced a kind of wild war-dance on the forehatch, vowing he would have blood for blood, while his cheeks blazed with two red spots and his bright eyes glared most wonderfully. Then the skipper told Salton to take the knife away. Harry suggested he should do it himself. Meanwhile I was edging up to Broome and put in a word, for I had a great deal of influence over him when he was mad like that, as I afterwards proved often and often in Melbourne. But he would not listen, and still flourished the knife. Now I don't know whether it was brave of me or only foolhardy, but I got behind him, put my arm round his neck and pulled him over backwards. The knife flew out of his grasp and was picked up, and when Broome was picked up too, he showed no irritation at the way I had served him. Then the captain commanded Salton to give up his weapon, which he promptly and most decidedly declined doing. As no one would volunteer to face the battery, the captain adopted another course, and told Salton to see that every one went below. He was very proud of his deputed authority, and I, having no wish to be pent up in the foul 'tween-decks until it pleased me to go there, had to jump up aloft to get out of his way. Then the captain and I escorted the mates to their respective bunks, and all was quiet except the gale, which was now at its height. I stood under the break of the poop and watched it for some time. It was now past five o'clock.

The sea was a wonderful sight, and the ship, as it drove through the waves with most of its sails torn in fragments, which whipped and knotted themselves into ropes on the yards, seemed like a flying creature tormented by strong invisible hands. The decks of the *Seringapatam* were continually full of water, and the main deck ports having been wrenched and beaten out, it was hazardous in the extreme to venture forward. Yet at such a time the captain's wife and the young girl passenger came out of the saloon on to the main deck.

Mrs. —— was as pale as death; the girl was flushed fiery red; both were most disgracefully intoxicated and could scarcely stand. I was really shocked beyond measure and ashamed; but being the only person then on the main deck, I did not think it right to allow them to stay in a place where even a sober man was in danger; so I opened the saloon door and pushed the girl in first, and after her the captain's wife, who fell down, and for a moment prevented me shutting the door. Just at that moment a heavy sea came on board and poured into the open saloon, thoroughly drenching the two women. I rolled the eldest in unceremoniously, and jamming the door to, left them struggling to rise.

I have got so far in the narrative, and in spite of what I said some pages back about my fearing lest some should disbelieve me, I have now to relate something still more incredible even to myself as I recall it, than any thing that I have yet written. Perhaps it is not quite impossible that a captain should obstinately stand to lose almost a whole suit of sails, although it is foolish enough, but that the same man should go below, when both his officers were drunk and incapable, and leave his ship to the care of the carpenter, who was not a sailor, seems like a fable. And yet it is just this that our skipper did. He ordered "Chips" to stay on deck from eight to twelve, and call him at midnight, and then coolly went below and turned in. At midnight the man duly summoned the captain, who did not turn out, and without waiting to be relieved, went to his bunk. Thus from twelve till two there was nobody on deck but the men at the wheel, for the Lascar whose look-out it was remained in the fok'sle, taking advantage of there being no officer of the watch. And we nearly paid a dreadful penalty for the criminal negligence our commander displayed. At three bells, or half-past one, the helmsmen were so near losing control over the vessel, that she almost came broadside on to the waves, and shipped a tremendous sea on the starboard side, as if the whole ocean were coming on board. I heard a terrific shock over my head, and then the rush and roar of the water as it washed over the rail, and poured down through every crack in the hatch into the 'tween-decks. It was some ten minutes before she cleared herself sufficiently of the sea for us to get on deck, and then we could see what had happened. The after boat on the starboard side, which had been lifted some ten feet above our heads by "skids" or "strongbacks," was lying on the deck in fragments, and the skids were smashed and splintered as well. Some well lashed 400-gallon tanks had disappeared overboard and with them the harness casks where the salt meat was kept; a kind of bridge, running from the poop towards the mainmast, which carried a large standard compass, had gone too, together with its valuable burden, and some of the iron stanchions, which were beaten and twisted out of all shape. The brass rail on the starboard side of the poop was gone, and the box where the signalling flags were kept. It was only the task of a moment to take this in with the eye, for there were loud bellows for help from the mate's berth. It seems that the wreck of the boat had been launched against his windows, staving them in, and admitting sufficient water to fill the berth up above the level of the highest bunk. The cold bath had roused him from his drunken slumbers, and he, fearing to be drowned like a rat in his hole, was imploring aid from all and sundry to help him to open his door, which was jammed hard by the great weight of water inside. It took three of us to release him, and then we went into the saloon, which was fairly afloat, for one of the doors had been burst open by the same sea. It was a melancholy sight and not a little disgusting, for the captain's wife was sitting in pronounced deshabille, in a foot of water, vowing she should be drowned, and imploring us to dive in, so to speak, and bring her to dry land. As for the captain, he was now on deck.

In the early morning, when I went up, although it was still blowing fairly hard, it was no longer a tempest, and the sea was rapidly subsiding. But the vessel looked a wreck, even if she had lost no spars, with the torn sails, the flying gear, the broken skids, and stove-in ports, while the second mate looked worse yet, being ornamented with two black eyes and innumerable scars. He grinned at me in a somewhat shamefaced manner, but said little. When Mr. Mackintosh came on deck I could have roared with laughter to see the two together eying each other as if to say, "He's rather worse than I am myself," and as if calculating how much difference in value there might be between two badly swelled lips and a nose apparently knocked on one side. But the Lascars, the very men who had beaten these two for trying to get them to work the day before, were now as obsequious as slaves, and hurried to do the bidding of their officers, without a smile on their faces, although I dare say they chuckled inwardly at the aspect of their superiors. I never knew if the captain reprimanded them, but I think not, as he was to blame for allowing every one to drink as much as he pleased, nor was his own conduct extremely praiseworthy, as any one, I think, will allow.

From that time forward, until we reached Melbourne, a fortnight later, everything went smoothly. There were no more rows and no more drinking matches. Mrs. —— came on deck as calmly as ever; the young passenger behaved as usual, the captain was as silent and quiet as before. And as for us, we prayed for land, without knowing what we were to suffer when we got there. For myself, I confess to feeling a strange chilliness about the heart when we anchored in Hobson's Bay and saw before us the distant city of Melbourne in the dust-coloured land which was to be our new home, and as I paced the decks of the *Seringapatam* for the last time, I was almost sorry to think that the assurance of daily victuals and nightly lodging, though both were vile, had come to an end, and that I was to shift for myself, like a young bear with all my troubles before me. And certainly there were many to come.

CHAPTER II.

IN MELBOURNE CITY.

I was just nineteen when I landed in Melbourne, and my stock in trade to succeed in life there was twenty-five pounds, a pair of hands, a good constitution and a general greenness which my experiences on board the *Seringapatam* had done but little to mitigate. And of course I had a batch of letters of introduction which did me one service at least, by ridding me of the illusion that the average man will go an inch out of his way to help a stranger. The only service rendered me was by a bookseller in a large way of business. He recommended me to lodge at the house of one of his clerks who lived at Emerald Hill, a suburb of Melbourne, thus killing two birds with one stone.

Most of my chums on board the vessel disappeared from my view at once. Roland and the

Yorkshireman went off to Geelong, where an English cricketing eleven was then playing one of the games in the first series of Inter-Colonial cricket matches. Cotton came ashore with ten pounds and spent it in two days on champagne and wild debauchery, starting on the third day to beg. Meeting me in Elizabeth Street he solicited a loan of a few shillings, being already on the downward path as far as his carefully tended personal appearance went. I gave him half-a-crown and some virtuous advice which he swallowed for the sake of the piece of silver. I did not see him for a week, and then he was glad to be lectured by a boy of nineteen for the sake of the sixpence which meant a "nobbler" of spirits. In the meantime I spent three days at Ballarat, as I hoped to obtain some work there from a man to whom I had a letter which promised more than the perfunctory business epistles I had brought from Manchester. But times in that bright, wide-streeted city of alluvial mines were not so brilliant as the sunshine: resembling rather the sombre foliage of the Australian forests I first marked on my hundred-mile railroad journey thither. I was kindly treated, but returned on the fourth day to my Emerald Hill home.

For some ten days I amused myself plodding about the city which untravelled colonials deem the finest in the world; I went down to Sandridge, visiting the *Seringapatam* to chat with the officers and the Malay bo'son; in the evenings I went to an occasional theatre, or spent an hour in the library in Swanston Street; the only thing I did not do was to look for work. And the necessity for that came earlier than it otherwise would have done when I met Roland and found him as he said "on his beam ends," without any money. He asked for some promptly, and got it from me without any reluctance. His appearance, his charm of manner, his real beauty, his experience of life, had a curious glamour for me. Even though I could not but be aware that his vivid imagination played tricks with the truth, it was with difficulty I refrained from believing his wildest and most improbable stories. He had that natural gift of convincing, which is the real charm of fiction: he believed himself. Our friendship increased with his necessity; finally I left my suburban lodging, and came to live with him in Queen Street, where I henceforth paid the bills. And though I had been almost penurious in my own expenses, my twenty-five pounds had by this dwindled to about five. When that was gone the necessity for work stared us in the face. But for labour of any kind Roland had an unconquerable aversion. He declared that he knew what it was, and infinitely preferred to defer the evil day by pawning everything he and I possessed. I for my part having never done any hard work was not so keenly set against it as I am now, and daily implored him to try it again.

One day when this pawnbroking business of ours

had almost run out, when even our empty portmanteaus were got rid of as useless incumbrances to our small bedroom, Roland and I met a friend of his from Leeds. Regardless of bystanders they danced a wild dance of greeting on the pavement, and then subsided into an animated series of questions. Tom had been in the colonies for four years, and after working up country on the Murrumbidgee, had come down to town with a cheque and some notion of returning home to become respectable. But Melbourne had been too much for him, and now he was working in the goods sheds of the Government Railway in Spencer Street, making six shillings a day for eight hours' work. It was there and then decided that we should also apply for work at the same place. Tom said that the timekeeper who hired the men each day was an Englishman, and very good to countrymen of his who were "dead broke," as he himself had been in the same condition. I found out afterwards that this railway was a kind of refuge for the destitute. Very many young Englishmen of good education worked there for a time.

That night I met a man who had been, like myself, an Owens College student in Manchester. He knew several friends of mine intimately, and though I had never met him in England his name and doings were quite familiar to me. He was a man of brains, but as I saw him seated on a table in a most disreputable drinking place, he looked very far on the road to ruin. He had been through a course of terrible debauchery at home, and showed no signs of reformation now. A great reader, he had an almost unexampled acquaintance with all that is vile in literature from Aretino upwards and downwards, and his conversation was full of reflected lights from this foul stream. He was going, so he said, to Tasmania as classical master in one of the best schools there. As I knew that he was not a very good classical scholar I looked somewhat surprised. He smiled as he noticed it, and instantly produced from bulging side pockets Roman after Roman in Giles's word-for-word translations. He told me with a chuckle that he believed he had a corner in this particular article, for he had bought every second-hand copy in the market. It seemed hardly likely that he would make his mark as a master. I never heard how he succeeded or what became of him after we parted that night. The next day I had plenty of other things to think of, for I did some hard work for the first time.

Roland, Tom, and I went down in the morning to the goods sheds, and took our places in a long double line of men waiting to be hired. The job was essentially day work; employment one day by no means implied employment on that following. So Roland and I would have stood almost as good a chance as Tom even if I had not had the enterprise to speak to the timekeeper beforehand. So fortunately we were all three taken on and were made sure of at least six shillings if we could stand eight hours' work. As the timekeeper beckoned to me and I walked out of the long ranks of some three hundred men, something of the same curious feeling came over me that I had felt when I first saw the brown and barren land about Cape Otway from the deck of the *Seringapatam*. I was going to

learn something new, and nervously doubted my strength and even my courage.

I was parted from Tom and Roland. They worked inside the shed. I was put outside on a platform where iron rods, machinery, bridge materials, tin plates, pig iron and fencing wire, were loaded for the upper country. We worked in gangs of four, two standing inside the truck to stow what the other two handed them. To my delight I found I was almost as strong as any of my new mates, and saw that with a little experience and harder hands I should do very well. Fortunately the work I had done on board the vessel had toughened me in some measure, so no one complained that I did not do my fair share of the job. Though by night I was of course very stiff and tired, I was curiously pleased with the knowledge that I really could earn my living with my hands. I had some of the conceit taken out of me next day when I found a difficulty in getting out of bed. Roland, who had come home grunting dolorously, was only too happy to persuade me that neither of us could work that day, and a watch, the last pawnable thing I had hung on to, enabled us to take a few days' more holiday. I admit I was nothing loth; but when it became urgent to work again I had to explain to the timekeeper that the first hard labour in my life had incapacitated me for awhile. Henceforward for three months I worked as regularly as possible; the only days I missed were those on which I was not hired.

During this period I handled all kinds of heavy merchandise, from pig iron to wheat, from thrashing machines to salt. Sometimes I worked in the sheds where beer and spirits were shipped, and saw the curious tricks men will use to get liquor without paying for it. Sometimes my mates purposely slung a cask of bottles of beer badly in order that it might slip and get stove in. Then they hid some of the bottles in piles of straw. Setting others to watch the man in charge they sometimes deliberately knocked the head out. I have often seen men lift up a small case of whisky and drop it on the stone floor. One of the bottles was sure to break, and then the escaping spirit was drunk as it trickled from the corner of the case held above the mouth. If any one got drunk he was discharged, but this seldom happened to the worst thieves, as they were experienced drinkers. As I drank very little at any time I never got into trouble, and liked working there, as the lifting was not so heavy as in the grain shed.

My companions were an odd mixture. Of course, they were mostly ordinary working men; but at times I got in a gang with educated young men, the ne'er-do-wells of very respectable families. Two sons of a consul-general often piled wheat with me; sometimes Tom was in my gang; and then I might get put with ruffians of the lowest order. Yet there was rarely any trouble, and in this my first experience I found it as easy to get on with such as I have done since. But some of the "gentlemen" had a bad time of it until they learnt only modesty could compensate for want of knack or strength or knowledge, and that respect among a crowd of democratic workers can only be earned.

During these months I was very fairly happy, and though I found continuous hard work by no means delightful, the pleasure of being idle in the evening was the more acute. It was only when I unloaded firewood and had to spend all my leisure time in the surgical extraction of splinters that I was really miserable. I cared nothing for the burning heat of that late summer, and worked even better in it than those who were more accustomed to the climate. Even a bitter black sandstorm, which drove us from work and sent me for shelter into a great tube that now makes part of the Echuca and Deniliquin bridge, was a new experience, and on account of its strangeness pleasant. As I grew hardened and knew my strength better I shirked no heavy lifting and was more than an average worker among the hundreds there. I began to get courageous, the town palled on me, the mystery of the up-country life enticed me. I began to plan leaving Melbourne.

For our pleasures, the pleasures which pleased Roland and Tom, irked me. An odd night in a hot theatre, packed in the sweltering pit, watching a third-rate English travelling company; evenings spent in Hosie's Bar in Big Bourke Street, even our Sunday's run down to Sandridge and the walk on the pier, lined on both sides by Australian clippers belonging to Money, Wigram, to Green and the other colonial traders, grew tiring, especially after my brother Cecil's ship, the *Soukar*, went off to England. He was then an apprentice, and as both he and I had to work we saw little of each other. When he was gone I determined to try the bush. But I found much difficulty with my two mates. Tom had been in the bush and did not like it; and as for Roland, his reasons for being contented where he was appealed very forcibly even to me, when I could stand outside and view matters on first principles.

I have said he did not like work; he owned it very frankly. And having had a slight accident to his foot during his second week's work in the sheds, he stayed at home, ostensibly to cure it, but in reality to carefully prevent its getting well. And during the time of his protracted convalescence I supported him. It was odd that he was always worse in the morning, when Tom and I went to work, but it was even odder that he should be well enough in the evening to go in for any amusement we could afford. In the course of very numerous professions, he had once been for a while a medical student. He pointed out to me as a curious pathological fact the morning and evening states of his injured foot, and complained when I was sceptical. This foot was his chief argument for staying in Melbourne; it was one of my chief reasons for getting away. Perhaps the country might do him good. For I had begun by now to lose some of the vivid greenness which characterized me on our first acquaintance. He taught as much as any one man might. So with some restrained irony, I lamented his sad case, and then without any irony at all, announced my intention of going up country—with him if he liked, but if not without him. I carried my point, and then Tom was ready to come too. I settled on Albury in New South Wales as our objective point, and pointed out to them that the Border City must after all be a very important place, and no bad substitute even for Melbourne. And having with some difficulty convinced them, if not myself, I set about saving as much as possible, in order to pay our fares to Wodonga, on the Murray opposite Albury, which was then as far as the railway went. And then what ought to have been a great aid to us became a hindrance. Tom's relatives in England were so ill-advised as to send him twenty pounds.

Until that twenty pounds was spent he would not budge. He ordered new clothes, refused to do any more work, went in for all kinds of amusement, as if he had received hundreds. Roland indeed magnified it into such, and procured for us all an amount of respect I had not calculated upon. He went round to all our haunts, proclaiming that each of us had received much money from England. I was tackled on all hands for loans, and though I was still at work in the sheds I had some difficulty in convincing our needy friends that my people had not sent me an unlimited amount of cash. One evening as Roland and I were sitting on our doorstep to enjoy the little air there was, Cotton came down the street, and recognizing us, sat down on the edge of the pavement. He had been the great swell of the *Seringapatam*, but now he was absolutely in rags. His toes protruded through his boots; his coat was buttoned and pinned up to his unshorn throat, to hide the absence of a shirt; his hat was ventilated in a manner never contemplated by its manufacturer, and yet in all this desecration of what might have been a fine man, there was a curious reckless *bonhomie* and merriness rarely seen in a confirmed drinker. He related his adventures without shame. He had begged of such an one; had procured money from a second, to take his clothes out of pawn; had victimized a third, and wound up by declaring that he knew every charitably disposed person of any eminence in the whole city. I gave him sixpence, and he went away very contentedly. When Tom came in I told him of this, and prophesied the like state for him if he did not mend his ways. But that twenty pounds had to be spent, and spent it was, with nothing to show for it but a new suit of clothes. What we could not show were things that yet left their mark—curious experiences on the shady side of life in Melbourne, which my quasi-classical friend of pornographic literature might have delighted in. For the inherent vices of the older civilization flourish and abound in the southern hemisphere. I was glad when by work, and the final selling of everything unneedful, I was able, with some assistance from our repentant friend Tom, to take three tickets to Wodonga, from the very station in which I once, as an odd job, cleaned carriages. It was about four in the afternoon when we started. We ran out of Melbourne into the bush.

At the best of times, even in the bright and glorious sunshine of its unclouded spring or summer noons, the Australian forest is melancholy with its sombre metallic green and scanty brown herbage under the lofty straggling trees. But now, under the circumstances, seeing that we were venturing into the unknown with so little money to spare, the scene was extremely fearful and dolorous to Roland, who reproachfully pointed out the barren look of the land. He sat in his corner prophesying dire events of starvation, of hardly-sought hard work, of thirst and death in days to come. He was a little maudlin. Gradually however by a process of continual imbibition from a concealed bottle, presented to him on his departure by a girl who served behind the bar in a little Melbourne hotel, he grew jocose and merry, persisted in throwing his coppers out of the carriage window for luck, took to singing sea shanties, and ended by bravely defying fate, accusing me of lack of enterprise in not having left town before. It was a relief when he fell asleep and remained silent, save for an occasional gurgle

until we ran into Wodonga at two o'clock in the morning. We took our bags in silence, and, cold, nervous and ill at ease, alighted in the dark terminus, knowing not whither to go. Among the three we possessed no more than twenty-two shillings and sixpence. We stood in the moonlight outside the station, as they turned out the lamps, in some dismay at the sombre solitude that surrounded us. Roland's courage had evaporated; he said bitterly "Is this your city?" There was not a house in sight. I myself was somewhat discouraged, until a friendly porter assured us that we could get rooms for the night at one "Baggy's," and volunteered to show us the way. We shouldered our baggage—a seaman's bag, an old portmanteau, and a large bundle—and followed him into the forest.

Even at this hour scarcely a scene in all my wanderings remains so vividly impressed on my memory. The sky was all but a cloudless void of a curiously transparent yet sombre turquoise. In its midst, not close against the sky background as in our home atmosphere, but detached and free in the immeasurable obscure of the heavens, shone a brilliant moon casting light of inconceivable intensity and shadows of almost startling blackness. The day before a sharp and sudden rain-storm had washed the solitary forest paths to white gravel that still held pools of gleaming water. The gigantic gum trees of the riverside stood up solidly defined against the heavens, but were not more material as it seemed than their distinct and apparently obstructive shadows. The atmosphere was sharp and chill, although there was not a breath of air to stir the lightest leaf or move what faint white threads of cloud mingled with a nebulous mist of stars. There was entire and absolute silence, for the river, though so close at hand, moved with the idle onward motion of a stream in a continent of plains. And it was long past midnight; the Australian world was all asleep. This was the bush as I first saw it; and as an anti-climax we came to Baggy's.

Poor Baggy was a man of Falstaffian dimensions, who afterwards came to an untimely end by falling out of a buggy on his head. Having stayed up on the chance of travellers coming in the last train, he made a hospitable supper for us at very reasonable prices. It was three o'clock ere we left the kitchen and marched some twenty yards through the moonlight to reach the house in which the bedrooms were. Tired as I was I did not remain awake to listen to Roland again reproaching me for bringing him to a wilderness, but fell fast asleep in the very middle of his doleful jeremiad.

CHAPTER III.

ON THE BANKS OF THE MURRAY.

In the morning we were all three in better spirits than we had been: a good rest in comfortable beds did its work even on Roland, who seemed the day before to think that he had for ever bidden sheets farewell. The day was brilliant, the season of the year late summer, and the first rains had freshened the dusty trees; when I went out I saw a bright green parrot flash past me, and going a little further I came to the river which here ran in a deep channel. By the time breakfast was over and our modest reckoning with our heavy host settled, we were eager to get to the border city of which we had heard such flourishing accounts. I for my own part only looked on it as a halting place until I could get some work in the bush. I was eager to learn all about horses and bullocks and sheep; I wanted to learn riding and the management of stock; the enticements of the shadowy and mysterious were upon me. But the others loved the flesh-pots of Egypt, and prayed for acceptable work in a luxurious town, such as I still hopefully painted Albury. Had I known as much as I do now of the methods adopted in new countries for booming new "cities" I might have discounted my own expectations. The imagination of a journalist owning town lots in a fresh location is poetic, he is truly a maker. And the omnibus, a very civilized omnibus, came from Albury to pick up any passengers who might come by the morning train from the south. We clambered on top, and in a few minutes rattled across the long wooden structure bridging the Murray. We were in New South Wales.

Though Albury has since grown to very respectable dimensions, it was then a straggling town with wide streets whose houses were placed at far intervals save in the business portion of the main thoroughfare. There were no bustling throngs in the thoroughfares; what people we saw seemed more interested in us than we expected; it was a bad sign that we attracted attention. Strangers in a money-making place receive little notice. For a few moments I repented my rashness in leaving Melbourne where a living at any rate was fairly certain. Hoping that this might not be the main city, that we were perhaps in a suburb, I inquired from the driver if this was the town. "And a very fine town too," was his answer. I avoided Roland's eye. We stopped at an hotel, and being treasurer I hired rooms as cheaply as possible, much to Roland's disgust, for though we now had no more than seventeen shillings and sixpence he wanted to act as a man of unbounded resources. After seeing our modest baggage, which alone would have marked us as sufficiently poor, placed in our rooms, we went out to view the town and discuss our prospects. As we went down the main street the little boys made audible and contemptuous remarks on us as "new chums"; one loafer at a corner told another that we were evidently run-away apprentices from some English ship. We climbed a low hill at the east end of the town, and sitting on the grass, contemplated Albury at our ease. I received a quantity of abuse from my two mates with desperate equanimity. But all the time of this dual tirade I could not help thinking that Albury was at least beautifully situated on the broad flat bounded by rising hills, and in the distance the Murray was silver bright.

Our prospects in this town were certainly not over encouraging. None of us had a trade; it is true we were able to work as labourers, but of these the home supply was quite equal to the demand. I had no thought of trying to secure a situation as a clerk; I had no hope of obtaining such a post, and moreover cared little for that kind of work. I had come up country to go into the bush, and did not want to drive a pen. I would rather tackle a team of bullocks. But I knew no way of getting such a job or anything similar to it, and I had not yet learned to put my blankets on my back and plunge into the unknown. Tom did all he could to discourage me from taking such a step. He enlarged on hunger and thirst, and told dire stories of men lost in the bush and never found, of the discovery of unknown dead men and sun-dried skeletons. At last I was as ready as either of them to rest awhile in town and learn something of the country before I ignorantly tried it. And though the obtaining of work seemed impossible, luck came to us very curiously.

A certain high dignitary of the English church, whom Roland once met in his father's house, had come to Albury the day before our arrival. We heard of this at the hotel dinner table. Without knowing whether he was still in town or not, Roland, who was in desperation, went off to the vicarage. Although he failed to see the greater man, for the good reason that he had returned to Melbourne, he so impressed the churchman whom he did see by his good looks, his plausible tongue, and his adventurous story, that he was forthwith invited to take up his quarters in the vicar's house.

He returned chuckling with joy, and jubilantly promised to help me in some way through his new friend. Two days afterwards I was installed as clerk in the office of a prominent stock and station agent, whom I have every reason to remember kindly on account of his amiability. As for Tom, nothing could be found to suit him, so he marched off up country with his blankets on his back, and a sovereign in his pocket. We heard from him in a fortnight. He had tramped through Wagga Wagga to Narrandera on the Murrumbidgee, and there found work. I have never seen him since.

For three months I lived a curious kind of triple life. Being rather poorly paid, I lodged in a house frequented by labouring men, workers of all descriptions, harness makers, bricklayers, plasterers, carpenters. Sometimes I shared my double-bedded room with one of these. One night my companion was a giant of a man who had done three years for cattle stealing. It was said that he was not the really guilty man, but had preferred to suffer rather than betray others. As I found him very kind and amiable, I do not care two straws if he did steal the cattle. It is an odd thing that there seems to be no particular aversion in the bush for such thieves, although in America every one is down on that particular form of crime, while man slaying is esteemed a comparatively venial offence, if indeed it is not looked on as a virtue.

I got on very well with these men. On one

occasion I was even chosen to act as timekeeper in a fight between two plasterers, who had had a preliminary rough and tumble in our eating room. The affair was settled on Sunday afternoon in the bush about half a mile away. In the evening I dined at the house of one of the town's bank managers. For though I was very poor and lived in such a place, it did not prevent my being to some extent in society, as far as there is any in a bush town. This bank manager's wife was a very well-read woman, and lent me a great number of books. Curiously enough she was a confirmed agnostic, though her husband was orthodox and a churchwarden.

My work in the office was light enough, and through meeting men who came in to buy and sell sheep, cattle, and horses, I began to get a little second-hand knowledge of bush life. I always kept in view the desirability of getting away from an indoor employment, for all that I heard made me more anxious than ever to know the really characteristic life of Australia. The walks I sometimes took by myself on Sunday into the bush tickled my imagination. Everything was so strange and new to me : the nature I had known in England was transformed into something utterly unknown.

Not very far from the town, on the side of a low hill bordering on the Murray, was a small clearing, or rather a naturally open space, where the woodcutter had never worked. It was on the way to or from nowhere, and by reason of a guardian ring of thick undergrowth, was unfrequented even by sheep or wandering cattle. There I, who had stumbled accidentally upon this happy spot, used to sit on a stone in the shadow of a box tree, and there the numberless bright birds of the sombre bush came to chatter and mock at me, all the time shrilling ear-piercing question or comment, from tree to tree.

It was my first acquaintance with vivid colour in wild birds. The first time I made my way thither I was startled by the hues and unexpected brilliance of the parrots and parroquets. I could not at once divest myself of the thought that some aviary of precious coloured and rare birds had been mischievously opened, to the unutterable grief and loss of some wealthy and indefatigable collector, and that these, the escaped denizens of his cages, had been brought together from all tropical climes about the equator. Their quick and tremendous shoots of flight, their sharp and various cries and human whistlings, their hurrying now here and now there, favoured my fantastic thought, for it seemed that they were in a high state of political excitement, as if something were to be done, and that quickly, in the new Republic of the Birds.

In the middle of my clearing was a small dead tree, in height about twenty feet, which had been gradually divested of both leaves and bark until it shone white against the dull metallic greens of the live forest. This tree was a convenient and conspicuous perch, and was seldom left untenanted, though not often occupied by more than one species

at a time. The birds who particularly affected it were the small bright green parroquets, who often fly in flocks of many hundreds. It was at first strange and startling to almost feel them flash past me within a yard's distance, screaming the while in deafening chorus, to see them go in a solid body at a terrible speed towards this tree as though they meant to break it in fragments, and then to watch them shoot up and settle in sudden silence, turning the gaunt white limbs to a branched vivid gigantic coral. Then as though in admiration of their own closed and shining ranks they kept quiet for a few moments, until another impulse sent them screaming into the bush like a thick flight of shot. And perpetually green changed to red, and red to mingled scarlets and greens all day long, so that this kaleidoscopic dead tree seemed something magical—a very chameleon among its living relations, that do not alter their colour till death robs them of their verdure once for all. I do not think it any wonder that I longed, for a time at least, to live in the real bush, at home with nature.

In truth the nomadic instinct was always strong in me, and even from my early childhood had been fostered by the exigences of my father's profession, which compelled him to change his place of residence at frequent intervals. It was difficult for me to be content for long in one spot. With the open prospect of long Australian distances I got uneasy. In a wild country we revert; the earlier knowledge and inherited experience of the race prick us on. The feeling is more or less universal; it is usually conquered by circumstances, by a lack of courage, or by that greedy knowledge of the purely advantageous in a conventional society which makes men successful and detestable at once. And I had no particular desire to be successful, but would rather follow my instincts.

One day as I was working, or pretending to work, in the office, the owner of a sheep station on the Upper Murray, some forty miles or so above Albury, came in to interview my "boss." In the course of conversation he said he wanted a boundary rider. Now a boundary rider is a man whose main duty it is to ride round the fences and see that they are in proper condition. If he finds them broken down by a horse, or a bullock, or if some heavy "old man" kangaroo has jumped short and smashed them, he repairs the gap. It was just such work as appealed to my imagination. "Would I do?" I asked suddenly. It appeared on questioning that I would not, as I owned that I had not been on a horse since I was a child. But when Mr. T—— returned to town a fortnight after he offered to give me a job at Dora Dora, if I liked to learn and do what I could, taking the small wages of ten shillings a week. As I could not believe I was worth more in my then state of bush ignorance I accepted his offer, and made arrangements to leave Albury at once. Roland lamented my departure, but as he was about to get a situation in one of the banks he was in very good feather, and showed no desire to accompany me in search of further adventures.

CHAPTER IV.

AT DORA DORA.

As I was not able to leave Albury until my employer found some one to continue my services as clerk, I was obliged to remain a few days after Mr. T—— returned to the station. Station in Australia is the universal equivalent for farm or ranch. When I was released I went up with a Mr. Mitchell to a house about ten miles from Dora Dora, and stayed there all night. In the morning Mr. T—— rode over, bringing a led horse for me. It was my first essay on horseback since the age of about nine, when I rode my father's horse bareback, and I had some slight doubts as to how I should come out of the experiment. It was rather rough on a new beginner that our road should be no road at all, and that the barely perceptible bridle path should lead at once to a complication of hills thick with brush and timber, tee-tree scrub and wattles. My stirrup leathers were too long, but as my new boss seemed in a hurry, I had no desire to make him pull up for me to shorten them, and if I let him get ahead it seemed anything but likely that I should find him again. Our road lay between two mountains, not of any great altitude certainly, but they were very steep, so steep in fact that the way was usually called the Tunnel; the heavy foliage made it sombre, though the sun shone brightly overhead. Still we went up and up. Now and again a few half-wild sheep scattered at our approach. If I had not been so terribly busy in keeping on I dare say I might have seen a kangaroo, for on this station they were always plentiful. But with preserving a balance and avoiding the sharp stubs of broken wattle branches, I had quite enough to do. When we crossed the ridge or divide, there was rather an increase of speed than otherwise. Skin began to come off the inside of my knees; I was already stiff. I cursed horseback exercise, and thought I had come to a very rough school. And then we suddenly burst out of the thicker scrub; we were at the foot of the hills. Across the flat lay my future home.

The station of Dora Dora has about eighteen miles of river frontage, and runs back from the

Murray some two or three miles. It was originally ranged over by cattle, but when wool rose greatly in price, as it did some years before I saw the place, the cattle were replaced by sheep. It was an unfortunate change, for "fluke" was deadly in the mountains. This fluke is a species of hydatid, and destroys the liver; the animals affected by it grow thin, pine away and die. Salt seems the only thing to prevent, or at least alleviate it, and prolong life. As I found out afterwards part of my work was to help to pack salt up into the mountains—for there are no natural salt or alkali licks there as in Western America. The sheep on the great north-west plains of New South Wales, whither I afterwards went, live greatly on a plant called the salt bush, and are always healthy.

The home station was close to the Murray, which here, at this season, was shallow and in parts fordable. It was but a stone's throw across, but still it ran very rapidly. The head of the navigable waters is Albury, whither steamers can come. The situation was very picturesque. Our garden—for the station had one producing fruit and vegetables —sloped rapidly to the river. Beyond that was a flat of many hundred acres, belonging to Thologolong Station, covered with dead and desolate gum trees which had been killed by ring-barking in order to allow better grass to grow. Beyond that again rose hills covered as on our side with wattles and the stringy bark which is so greatly used for roofing in the bush. So much I could note as we rode across the home flat. I was intensely glad to alight. My first lesson in horsemanship was assuredly a rough one; but on the whole, considering the country we had ridden over, I was not displeased with myself.

The position I occupied on this station was rather an anomalous one. I was not a regular hand— neither a rouse-about who is expected to do everything he is told, nor a boundary rider who considers it time to take his cheque if he has to handle anything but horses or a tomahawk when mending a brush fence. As I lived in the house, not at the men's hut, I was something like what is known in the bush as a "colonial experiencer," although I was paid, and such usually pay to be allowed to learn something, or nothing, about stock and the management of it. These are frequently young gentlemen whose friends can do nothing with them in England, and consequently pay some sheep or cattle owner to take charge of them and teach them the business, either as a preliminary to washing their hands of them completely, or to setting them up with sufficient capital to engage in pastoral pursuits for themselves. As a rule such an one does nothing but loaf about on horseback. I on the contrary, though I did live in the house, was expected to earn my money first and learn what I could afterwards.

For one thing, to my horror, I had to learn something about butchering. Two days after my arrival Mr. T—— took me down to yard, caught a sheep, killed it, bade me watch him skin it, and when it was done told me he expected that I now knew how it was managed. The whole unsavoury business took him some ten minutes. Three or four days later I received orders to kill another. I bribed Jack, the boundary rider, to do the actual murder, for a plug of tobacco. He regarded me somewhat contemptuously, telling me I should soon get over my delicacy, and then rode away. I began with the knife to operate on the dead sheep. In about half an hour I was covered with blood, but the skin was pretty nearly where it was when I began. I lighted

my pipe, took a rest and a smoke. Then I began again. I could not remember a single thing. One might as well have asked a first year's medical student to tie the subclavian artery. I got the wretched carcase into such a state that I actually felt remorseful. And then when the ghastly operation had lasted almost two hours Mr. T—— rode up. He looked over the fence calmly and asked what I had there. I replied that it was a sheep. He asked if a dog had been worrying it. Not that I knew of, was my reply; and then, sparing me further satire, he tied his horse up, took off his coat, and showed me where I had gone wrong. I never did so badly again, and long afterwards found that lesson useful.

My progress in horsemanship was not marked by anything so ludicrous; for one thing I found that I took to it quite naturally, that I was built more or less well for it. Certainly a few tumbles in jumping big logs and brush fences made me less conceited when I began to fancy that I knew as much about riding as Jack the boundary rider. Jack was always anxious to get me on a buck-jumper, and greatly lamented that there was no horse in the station who bucked satisfactorily, even after being turned out for a long rest. But what with running up the horses to the stockyard every morning, with going after our old bull when in spite of a log to his leg he managed to get into a small cultivation paddock, and with a little odd boundary work, I began to ride fairly well even before the winter or rainy season was over and the mustering of the sheep for marking began. But one day I had an experience which might well last a man the rest of his life. It was not through my bad horsemanship, but my ignorance of the country, for early one morning as I was going full gallop after a horse in thick scrub, I rode into a wire fence. This, as I found out afterwards, had been put up in a most unlikely place to find such a thing, and yet was necessary. It ran in a curve close to the river, where there was a ford. When the water was low the horses constantly went across to the other side, but of this I, as a comparatively new comer, had never heard. The horse and I fell together on the other side of it, for the top wire broke, and the others knocked my mount's legs from underneath him. Fortunately the ground on the falling side was soft, otherwise my leg would have been broken. As it was I escaped with some very bad bruises, and the horse with far fewer cuts than might have been expected. Though after these experiences I began to think I could ride, every now and again something happened that showed me I was still a new chum. For of driving bullocks I knew nothing, but Mr. T—— put me in the way of learning.

That day's adventures were sufficiently comical and irritating. I am no very great believer in the sagacity of animals, nor do I think that the four beasts I went to work with were any cleverer than the usual run of bullocks, but, nevertheless, the quickness with which they discovered that my knowledge of driving such an outlandish team was practically *nil* really amazed me. My "boss," a man of a somewhat taciturn if satirical turn of mind, who always took my knowledge and ability for granted until he discovered by the results that he had overestimated my powers, told me curtly one morning to yoke the bullocks up and haul in some firewood. And with this he rode away, leaving me in about as puzzled a state of mind as I should have put him in had I been in a position to order him, under divers pains and penalties, to translate a portion of Macaulay into immaculate Ciceronian Latin. However, I had my orders, and I meant doing something to show that I had at least attempted what seemed like the impossible. When the four bullocks, who indeed were very worthy and quiet animals, were safely in the yard, I commanded them in such gruff tones and with such oaths as I had heard used in like cases to arrange themselves and deceived by my delusive show of experience and authority, the two leaders, Spot and Baldy, placed themselves meekly in the required juxtaposition. But by the time I had fixed the yoke on the neck of Spot, the off-side bullock, both had discovered by the awkwardness of my movements that I was a most fraudulent novice, and as such to be treated with contempt. In spite of all I could do—and that was little enough—they decided on separating at once, and the yoke was left hanging on Spot's neck as he eyed me with mild contempt, while Baldy, the unencumbered one, who was of a more lively turn of mind, galloped gaily round the yard. I seized the whip, but instead of the heavy report which comes from it in a practised hand, my loudest cracks were manifestly feeble. It took me quite half an hour's exercise to reduce Baldy to a more subdued turn of mind, but at last I yoked them together securely. As I was eying them with a gentle sense of triumph, born of difficulties subdued and a new feeling of power and accomplishment, they turned their heads together with a quick movement, made a sort of duck, and faced right round with the yoke upside down. They had "turned the yoke," a very common and provoking trick among working bullocks, and one which sometimes can only be prevented by tying their tails together. It was a heart-breaking task to have to remove the yoke and replace it, for Baldy was so elated at my inability to flog him in a convincing manner that he was worse to handle the second time than the first. But at last I got the whole four yoked up, and even succeeded in attaching them to the waggon inside of half an hour, and we started off. Presently we came to a gate, which I opened for my slow-moving team to pass through without any particular misgivings. But, unhappily, the road turned short to the left, and as I failed to keep the "polers" well to the right, the wheel caught the gate-post, and in spite of my frantic objurgations, which probably they took for an exhortation to pull, they bent their necks to the yoke and ripped the post fairly out of the ground. With it about a rod of fencing came to grief. I looked at it woefully enough and set to work at repairs, the team having come to a standstill in the meantime.

When I had made things look a little less forlorn, I started again, wondering very much what was going to happen at the next gate, which was about a quarter of a mile away. On reaching it I halted, made all sorts of very careful calculations about the width of the way in and the distance between the posts, and then—pulled up the one on the off-side, or right hand! I confess to feeling very bad about it. My boss might not think so much about one gate, but to destroy two looked far too much as if I made a rule of it, and that I knew would not be passed by in silence. As I stared at the devastation I had caused, my four bullocks, whom I now began to hate with a pious and fervent hatred, went boring along with their heads down, as if nothing out of the way had occurred, and I had to run after them, using all sorts of strong language to induce them to stop. By the time I had propped up this second gate it was nearly noon, and noon was my dinner-time. But I determined to bring back some wood if it took me all day, and although my appetite was good, I staved off the pangs of hunger with a pipe, and made a third start for the woods. Up to that time I had at any rate had a clear road save for the two gates, but when I got among the timber I found my real difficulties had commenced, for though I succeeded in uprooting two or three stringy-bark saplings, and in snapping a young wattle-tree off at the stump, I presently found four bullocks totally insufficient power for me to make my way forward with the same disregard for obstacles I had hitherto displayed. In fact I got the waggon jammed between two large box-trees of about three feet in diameter, and they obstinately refused to be pulled up by the roots or to break short off to please me or any one else. I tried to back the bullocks, but they scorned me utterly, in spite of the Australian language I used. I might be as gruff as I liked, but I could *not* crack the whip, and their hides seemed as tough as the general situation. However, at last I succeeded in irritating them, which was something at any rate, and just as I had made up my mind to do what I should have done at first—that is, take them out of the waggon and pull it out backwards—they turned short to the right and broke the pole. On finding themselves free they started for home, but before they had gone ten yards hitched themselves to a large sapling by the chain, and got so tangled up that I could hardly tell which was which. And just then I spied my taciturn boss riding up. He would undoubtedly have been justified if he had exhibited some anger, but he only surveyed the scene with a subtle smile that made me far more uncomfortable than the expected volley of oaths, which I should have doubtless returned, but that smile was a weapon I could not match in my armoury of defence. Said he presently, "Do you know anything about bullocks?" "Yes, sir," I answered meekly. He stared at my presumption. "Pray, when did you learn it?" he inquired.

"This morning, sir," I replied more meekly than ever, and I really think I had him there. At any rate, he got off his horse, took the whip, disentangled the team, and dislodged the waggon without further words. We went home to dinner in silence, and I spent the afternoon at gate-repairing. That was my first experience in bullock-driving, but it was by no means the last, and though I never was very good at it, yet I managed as a general thing to get through eleven gates out of twelve without any very humiliating disaster.

The nomenclature of bullocks is sometimes very curious, and not infrequently brings into prominence the peculiar characters of their owners. One old fellow I heard of possessed four, which he named, with a lingering memory of ancient days when lucifers were not, "Flint," "Steel," "Tinderbox," and "Strike-a-light." It was once my lot to work for a squatter who rejoiced in a very odd name, and though upon the whole I retain very pleasant recollections of him, he managed in some way to excite the enmity of a neighbouring "cockatoo," as the smaller landowners are called, and by way of subtle revenge and irritation this man named one of his bullocks after the object of his aversion. It was done with the sole object of bullying and abusing it when the squatter rode by, and the poor animal, who certainly was not particularly objectionable, came in for a quantity of blows and dishonouring epithets, which he had not fairly earned, by serving as a whipping-block or scapegoat for the real or imaginary crimes of his human namesake.

Far more pleasing to me than bullock-driving, as implying less manual labour, was mustering the sheep in the higher ranges when lamb marking came due. We were always on horseback early and away from the homestead before the heat began. Riding through the river flats we passed the mightier gum trees, red and blue, and on the first slopes of the hills the golden wattle, with its brilliant masses of pure yellow, sent a heavy odour that rose and faded away and swelled again on the wind like some strange musical instrument whose notes appealed to another sense than that of hearing. Then came the rougher paths, narrow and thick set with scrub and the entanglements of brush, until we burst through them at last, and came out on opener greyer plateaus where a few lofty white gums shone like lighthouses. They gleam with a mealy substance that comes off like dry flour, and sometimes their old bark, stripping itself from the tree, hangs over in long fine curves, reaching even to the ground. For the Australian trees clean themselves yearly, casting off their outer integuments like the snakes which are so plentiful in their country.

When we were on the plateau the company usually separated after appointing a meeting place on some lower flat, and the sheep hunting began. In this mountainous land they grow very wild; numbers often escape the yearly shearing; in every clip are some long fleeces which have grown more than their customary period. So good dogs are above all essential to anything like a clean muster. We had all qualities with us.

So far as I am acquainted with both countries I should say that one essential difference in the handling of sheep in Australia and in North America is that of the use of the dog. The sheep dogs in the West are of the poorest quality; at any rate I never saw either in Texas or California one that an Australian shepherd would dignify with the name of dog at all. There the men working with sheep delight in having well-bred animals, and devote immense care and patience to their education. Their dogs are always collies—called by the way in the bush *coolies*—they come very often from good imported strains, and are frequently exceedingly handsome and clever. The price of a good one runs that of a horse very close. Indeed I have seen many very fair horses sold for five pounds, but never a sheep-dog of any reputation. I have heard fifteen pounds asked for a thoroughly trained slut on Dora Dora, and refused. There is no doubt that such prices rule owing to the fact that the distemper is very virulent in the colonies, often destroying half a promising litter. Yet when I was there hydrophobia was quite unknown, and most carefully guarded against at the ports.

The training of the puppies commences as soon as they are able to walk. In the bush, being of course on a sheep station, they usually see some of their future charges every day, and as soon as they are able to run well and bear the fatigue they go out with the older dogs. The first day I went mustering on Dora Dora I rode with a man named Stewart, the owner of the valuable slut I spoke of above. Flo came with us of course, and with her was a young dog puppy of hers. I could not help thinking that as far as knowledge of sheep went I occupied much the same relation to Stewart as the puppy did to his mother, and just as he willingly told me all he knew, and checked me when I was about to do wrong, so the experienced slut treated her son. She took care that he never headed the sheep off, and encouraged him with a glad bark when he did right. Busy as she was at times she never took her eyes, or at least one of them, off him, and evidently would have felt disgraced if her master had had any just cause to rate him. But when we had managed to get about a thousand or twelve hundred together, and had them headed down a gully towards the appointed *rendezvous*, well under command, she suddenly disappeared. I asked Stewart where she had gone, and he answered that he did not know but that she would probably turn up directly. About half an hour afterwards, just as we were debouching on to the little flat, where some other sheep already were, we saw a small mob of about two hundred and fifty apparently coming of their own accord to join ours.

But behind them was Flo. She had noticed them in the distance when bringing the others part of the way down, but evidently distrusting her son's capabilities of managing the larger number until they were well in hand and near their destination, she had waited her time to go after them. She was always ready to take charge of any number for hours together, and we could be quite sure that none would stray while she was round. There was no other dog on the station who knew the country as she did; though it was a mass of hills she seemed acquainted with every gulch about it.

When as far as could be seen we had cleared the disturbed quiet of the hills and massed the sheep together, we took them to the station and put them in the yards. In the morning all hands were down there early. Stewart, and the boss and another man stood against a dividing fence, and the younger hands, of whom I was of course one, caught and held the wretched little lambs for the surgical operation. The ear-mark that differentiated them legally from the property of the neighbouring squatters was made quickly and skilfully, and by each man's feet grew up a pile of dissevered tails. Let loose again the hurt and astonished animal ran bleating to its mother, who seemed so glad to have it back at any price that she could not trouble over an injury which in her own case had been long ago forgotten. And I jumped here and there all day long in a yard which grew hotter and hotter, and dustier and dustier still, till half blinded with sweat, and smarting with the yolk from the wool, I was glad for the sun to sink behind the hills. That at any rate hinted at the end, if it did not yet come, for though the Australian station working day is from sunrise to sundown, in the hills one cannot quite know when the due work is done as one may upon the long and level plains.

When all the marking was over there was a comparative rest. Shearing did not come yet awhile and I was freer to attend to the fences, some of which were put under my charge when Jack went. For, like many bush workers, he had made quite enough money for a spree, and was ready for it. Yet Jack only went down to town to "blue his cheque" at reasonable intervals. We had a quaint, worn down, half-worn-out old man on the station whom we considered a German. As he never said so and was known as Tom, and moreover spoke without any particular accent, I do not know what reason there was for thinking him a Teuton. But his sprees came off regularly about once every three weeks. He was absent for about five or six days over at a grog-shanty not far from Mr. Mitchell's, on the other side of the Tunnel, and then would turn up again and go to work. One day I was helping him at some work—if I remember rightly we were together remedying the effects on gates and fences of my first lesson in bullock-driving. Suddenly, thinking of England, I said half to myself, "*Eheu fugaces*," and then this blear-eyed old nondescript added quietly, "*Postume, Postume.*" I started and stared at him. He looked up in a queer melancholy way and said, "Why not?" It turned out that he knew far more of the classics than I could dare boast of; his knowledge of French and German seemed good; and even then, after many years of never seeing a mathematical book, he could talk Binomial Theorem, the Theory of Projectiles, and Geometry until I felt like asking him to give me a few lessons. But his history I never learnt, nor did I ask what I knew must be melancholy. Yet it was doubtless a human document.

Perhaps indeed I had little time to earn his confidence, for save when upon the back ranges riding round the fences with the sign of my work, a sharp tomahawk, slung to the dees of my saddle, I had little leisure. But I loved to be on the hills early in the morning after being roused at dawn by the laughing-jackass birds, who sat on the trees by the river, uttering their weird cacophony of human and asinine voices in satiric juxtaposition as though they mocked mankind in general. Riding up the creeks often a dense flock of white cockatoos flew overhead uttering the most ear-piercing screams. They followed me at times for half a mile until I wished for a gun to give the survivors some reason to deafen me with reproaches. Getting clear of them at last I often came to places which, save for a hint of a

track, seemed as primitive as if a wandering white man had never set his foot in this undiscovered country. Sometimes when in no hurry I tied my horse to the fence or a sapling, and going but a few hundred yards into the bush on a voyage of exploration, I came occasionally upon the ancient camping grounds of the grey kangaroo. It required a certain lightness of foot and deftness of tread to make one's way under the trees and through the scrub, without alarming them by the snapping of a dry twig or some unwonted rustle; but once, at least, I succeeded in watching for some minutes a dozen or more as they grazed or took their *siesta* in a small natural clearing in the utmost security of imagined loneliness. At such times there is a certain parodied humanity about them which those who only alarm or hunt them can never hope to see, for some of the larger ones standing up in the brush seemed like sentinels, while others lying at full length on their sides suggested a bivouac, or rather a peaceful picnic party. The scene was idyllic: these seemed like satyrs, those half-hidden like hamadryads, as the sunlight piercing through the trees into their shadowy camp touched them with light and dark, that made them obscure of form and outline. Perhaps if I had been older and more thoughtful I might have retreated in such guarded silence as I came, leaving them undisturbed in their haunts of ancient peace for very love of their sweet and natural simplicity; but

I was not so kind, and one shout was like a bombshell dropped into a party of soldiers. At a leap the young ones, the little joeys, were in their mothers' pouches, those lying down rose on the instant and each made a plunging jump into the nearest cover. A repeated "crash, crash," at regular intervals told of their hurried retreat in the opposite direction. They never made a mistake as to the location whence the sound that alarmed them issued. Then I returned to my horse, to find him with pricked up ears, wondering what had happened to make me yell in that way. And I went on homeward, every now and again cutting down a sapling or two to put on a low place in the fence. Or if I felt very lazy I promised myself to do it the next time I came that way, and returned home at a slow pace through the heavy silence of the forest, which was only occasionally broken by kangaroos or the startled trot of some wild horse—a 'brumby' who had escaped the rope and branding iron. The true wild horse that has been foaled by a wild mother is rare in this comparatively settled part of the bush, but once they ranged on the plains of New South Wales in thousands. It was a speculation to catch them and a business to shoot them. The method of destroying them by the rifle was ingenious. Long after leaving Dora Dora I met a man who for a time earned his living by killing warrigals. For, independent of the value of the hide, they are a great nuisance to squatters. The stallions came to the station at night, took away all the mares, and scared the geldings to death. These would be found in the morning trembling with terror in the stockyard. Any mare that was hobbled and could not go fast the stallion often bit and kicked, not understanding the nature of the impediment which prevented her galloping. So it was necessary to catch or kill these horses.

To do this successfully the hunter found out some favourite feeding ground, and, on getting within easy range under good cover, he aimed at one of the mares. At the sound of the shot the rest fled, the stallion bringing up the rear. But in a moment he would notice that one was missing. Increasing his pace he shot ahead of his harem, rounded them up and drove them back to the dead mare. Her he bit to rouse her from her untimely sleep. Finding this fail he often wheeled round and kicked her. Then another mare fell to the hunter's rifle. This flight and return sometimes occurred again and again, and each time a good marksman brought down one of the mob. If he had killed the stallion at first he would have secured but one, for the mares without his obstinacy could escape. Nowadays however the wild horse is getting scarce even in the northern plains.

Yet I ran a "brumby" in on Dora Dora after a long and exciting chase. Occasionally I had to go to one of the riverside paddocks which was about three miles round, and a perfect nightmare to a

G

horseman if there were any necessity for speed. The ground in no place was level, and through it rocks cropped up in every direction, here and there were small deceitful swamps as well as cup-like hollows masked by brush and scrub, while every now and again in a gallop one was confronted by a regular abattis of fallen interlocked timber, whose broken jagged branches protruded, threatening to stake the horse or impale the rider. One day on going to run up three horses feeding in this paddock I found a stranger. He was too wild for me to get near enough to see whether he was branded with some squatter's mark, but from the long main and lengthy tail falling away from its rump in the graceful curve characteristic of a warrigal, I judged that no man had ever had his hands upon it. I should have left this horse alone had it not been that its presence and example made the others as wild to approach as if they too had never been broken. The stranger attempted to leave the paddock at the place he had entered it. But he was fairly pounded as the take off was everywhere up hill, and the brush fence was very high. I started the chase. My objective was a little stockyard in an angle of the fence. Three times we went round the paddock at a breakneck pace. Once my horse stumbled and fell, but I lighted clear of him on soft ground without losing the reins. At last I ran close up to the four and began to think I was getting command of them, when suddenly the leader doubled to the left round some thick scrub. Now it is the nature of a stock-horse to endeavour above all things to prevent what he is chasing from getting away by any such manœuvre, and the one I rode cut instantly to the left also, increasing his pace as he did so. He picked his own place in the scrub, leaving me to take care of myself, which I did by dropping my face to his withers, putting my arms before my head at the same time. This is always the best way to charge thick scrub. In this position we burst through the bushes like a tornado, scattering the broken branches and leaves in all directions, and then just in front of us was a regular stockade of fallen timber. I had no time to think; before the dust was out of my eyes the danger was past, but I had just one sickening moment as my horse rose in the air. He jumped right through the branches of a fallen tree as I dropped to escape a sharp spear-like stub. Next day I went to look at the place, and found that there was absolutely no other way out of the *impasse*. The judgment of the experienced animal I rode was good: hesitation would have been fatal. Even a stock horse, accustomed as he is to stopping suddenly, could hardly have pulled up; and mine was in such a state of excitement which would have made him prefer killing himself to letting the other go. And on the next round the warrigal's wind and courage failed him. I drove him into the stockyard at last.

Soon afterwards I left Dora Dora after some

little trouble with my "boss," in which I was to blame. The same morning I had a fight in the garden with another young fellow working there, in which he showed a curious philosophy. After the exchange of a few blows we locked, and he came down undermost. "Don't let's make fools of ourselves," said he, as he reached for his pipe. I let him rise, remarking if that was the view he took of the situation I was quite content. Evidently, as they say in America, he was not a hog. He knew when he had enough. That afternoon I packed up my clothes in a rough kind of "swag," or bundle, and "humped" it down to Albury, reaching there on the following day. It was the first but not the last time that I "humped my swag." For on Dora Dora I was a kind of half-aristocrat, neither a do-nothing, nor a regular hand. Henceforward I threw gentility to the winds, came down to my bearings, and started as one who had learnt something and thought himself worth at least the regulation pound a week and his grub.

CHAPTER V.

THROUGH THE BULL PLAINS.

On reaching Albury I put up at the same hotel to which Roland, Tom, and I had been taken when we first crossed the Murray from the land of the Victorian "gum-suckers" to that of the New South Wales "cornstalks." As I had, besides the money I brought down with me from Dora Dora, some twenty pounds sent me from England, I was able to present a respectable appearance in town. So I went across and called at the vicarage, there learning that my wild friend Roland Broome was engaged in the peaceful pursuits of a bank clerk. I wondered how long it would last, for I knew he was apt to break out at times. Yet he had behaved himself as far as I could learn with an almost exemplary sobriety; that is to say, with the exception of a little drinking bout when on a visit to Corowa, some forty miles west of

Albury, none of the ladies in Albury had anything against him. Indeed, with all the younger ones he was more than a favourite. He was overjoyed to see me, and I had much difficulty in preventing my return from being the occasion of the loss of his precarious character. He described himself as the happiest man in the universe, declared he was in want of nothing, swore vigorously that New South Wales people were the nicest in the world, that he lamented not having known the country years before, and finally thanked me, with a variety of new and old expletives, for having been the occasion of his coming to a land where his virtues were appreciated. He certainly was a most fascinating and amusing man even when we were in poverty, when we lived in a low quarter of Melbourne and ate at a sixpenny restaurant; but now in prosperity, he bloomed and blossomed into fun and amusing anecdotes, which required all my knowledge of his fertile imagination to reduce to some credibility. He gave one evening on the verandah of the hotel a highly-coloured account of our passage in the *Seringapatam* which was so absolutely new to me that I remonstrated with him in private. But as all the listeners laughed till they cried he was perhaps justified. Certainly he made an experience seem amusing to me which was no joke even to remember.

I stayed in town about ten days. The summer was now coming in fast, and if I delayed departing I might lose all chance of work in the sheep-shearing which was about to commence. So I made preparations to set out on my journey by buying a horse. And though I flattered myself that I could now stick on with a certain degree of confidence in myself, I was most abominably swindled in my purchase. I had paid so much attention to mere equitation, that of the horse's anatomy I knew nothing. Soundness was a desirable quality, that was certain, but how to be even approximately sure that a horse was not screwed in every leg, I knew not. So a certain Englishman, who was probably not above taking a commission, persuaded me to buy my horse from a rascally Irishman who would have sworn his way through all the stone walls in Galway if there were the price of a creel of turf on the other side of his perjuries. I parted with £10 of good money and got a very bad mare. It is true she was in fine condition and shone like silk, but she was badly screwed in the near foreleg, and likely to break down any minute, as the hotel stableman told me with pity for my English ignorance. But in the morning of the next day I set out on my journey heading west down the main river road towards Corowa. I reached that town on the following day early in the afternoon, and then rode into the bush, taking the north road towards the Bull Plains.

In my time in Australia, some twelve years ago, there was little difficulty in a traveller getting sufficient to eat without paying for it, if he could manage to keep off main roads or very frequented tracks. Numbers of men in the bush never do any work at all but travel the year round, taking care to come to a station at "sundown," when there is no chance of their perfunctory application for work being entertained till the morning. After two meals and a good rest it is easy to be dissatisfied if any job is proposed, and the "sundowner" or tramp makes his way to another station. The usual formula is to ride up, and say to any one handy, "Can I see the boss?" The "boss" comes out. "Any chance of a job, sir?" Probably the answer is in the negative. Then, "I suppose I can stay here to-night?" This is, or was, rarely refused, and if the manager or owner is a good fellow he does not mind the traveller's horse going in the horse-paddock, provided of course that there is a fair quantity of grass, otherwise he has to hobble him and let him pick what he can where he can find it.

About noon on the day I left Corowa I came to a small station in a little plain surrounded more or less by pine scrub. As it was obviously dinner time by my sensations I rode up, and alighting, went to the biggest house or hut to find some half-dozen men eating, their sleeves turned up and their hats on their heads. When I asked for the boss no one would own to being the individual. "In fact," said the cook, "we're all bosses just now, the old man has gone into town." He invited me in, and I sat down with them to a tin dish of mutton, and a bucket of tea from which I scooped my

pannikin-full as if to the manner born. After dinner I set out again. The sun was very powerful, and the hotter it grew the worse became the day pest of Australia, the common fly. They swarm everywhere in the warm weather, get into one's eyes, ears, and mouth, and worry the horse to death. Of mosquitoes I had as yet had no very painful experience.

In this heat I travelled only slowly: for one thing I feared to fatigue the mare, though she showed no signs of giving way. I had continually to unhook my canvas water-bag from the saddle and take a drink, and was glad on passing another house to get it refilled. This water-bag should always be a traveller's companion. It may save him much suffering, save him even from death, if he gets "bushed," losing his way in a comparatively trackless country. If it be made of sufficiently porous canvas to allow the water to moisten the outside its contents are always cool, for the evaporation is rapid. A large one hanging under the verandah of a house is very commonly seen in the bush; and when the heat is sufficient to make water kept in any ordinary vessel quite tepid, a cool drink from a canvas bag may well rank as a luxury. But presently the sun began to decline. I had forgotten to ask at the last house where the next one was, and I foresaw I should probably have to camp out. When the sun went down without any signs of a station near at hand, I looked for a suitable place. Then I saw a fourwheeled buggy coming towards me drawn by two horses which were evidently much fatigued. When I reached it the driver pulled up, asking me how far the next house was. "About seven miles," I replied, and asked him a similar question. The last place he had passed was also about seven miles away. It was evidently a question of our picking a camp. We settled to stay together. I was without food, but he had enough for two. We hobbled

the horses and turned them adrift, and I set to work making a fire, by no means an easy thing to do in a country which was just there almost without wood. But by careful search I managed to collect enough to boil the "billy," or tin pot, which is even more useful and more universal than the water-bag. We ate a very frugal meal, and after a couple of pipes over the embers of the fire I paid him for his food by sharing my blankets with him. As it threatened to be rather cold, I only took off my boots.

I shall always remember that night, not because of anything startling that occurred—there was indeed no convulsion of nature, no storm, no eclipse, or earthquake. But it was a new experience; it was the first time I ever camped out under the arch of the skies, without even the shelter of a tent. Since then I have watched, all alone, the sun set on a vast and level plain on which I and my horse were the only living things to be seen. I have camped in the deserted beds of ancient rivers, in thick and choking brush, on the solitary summits of mountains, in dark cañons, on sweet prairies, listening half the night to the melancholy howling of coyotes and wolves; in dense forests among snow, and by waters that ran from glaciers thousands of feet above my couch; and yet in all these places and the thousand other that a wanderer for years sleeps in, I was never so moved as when I lay down on the desolate road which led northward to the unknown plains. As we thought would be the case the night grew chill, the southerly wind was searching after the hot day, but I did not trouble about that. I had begun a new life. Or was it indeed but an old one, one that my far ancestors knew before they settled in cities and devoted themselves to the rearing of an unnatural civilization?

In the morning after breakfast my companion presented me with the remainder of his provisions, and we parted, I northward, and he southward to Corowa. I passed the station which he told me was seven miles distance, and shortly afterwards another. Having food, I satisfied my noon hunger with that, filled my water-bag, and went onward to another sheep station. I began to come out upon the more open country. The scrub grew scantier, the trees fewer, from one thin belt of timber to the next was farther still and still farther. And now let me sketch you the sunlit plains of this Australian Riverina.

The road before me was but an indicated half-beaten track of brown earth; it dwindled in far perspective to a streak, and was lost in the haze that lay upon the horizon. Above the low and level skyline the heavens were faintly tinged with pale purples which only gradually yielded to the intense and perfect blue, and high overhead, so high as nearly to touch the zenith, the sun at noon seemed slow to move from the post where he held the w rld at such an advantage. The grass which had been green but a month ago was almost as sere and sapless as sun-dried twigs, and in parts already discovered the bare soil, for the white and dusty sheep in the shadows were many for the pasture in which they grazed. The trees under which they stood panting, with the outsiders drooping their heads lower and lower yet to catch the scanty shadow of their companions, were boxes, whose dull, metallic, blue-green leaves were powdered with faint fine dust, lifted even by the lightest air, or raised high by the tramping of the sheep as they moved from their noonday camp. The other trees were but scrub pines of a lighter green, too thickly set for anything but a stray dingo to make his way through, and too small to be of use to man, save perhaps to replace the broken whip-handle of some wayfaring bullock-driver.

It was a dry land that was for ever threatening thirst, for it could boast of but little permanent water. There were no perennial springs and creeks such as gladdened the thick shadows and cool places of the Murray Hills whence I had come, and the dug tanks which contained the winter's water were some of them already tainted by the odour of the yoke and grease of the sheep that frequented them, which even boiling and much tea could scarcely disguise or palliate. I myself had a bitter enough experience of drought before I came to the Big Billabong, for I was for more than twenty hours without sufficient water, after I had passed into that peculiarly characteristic series of plains ringed with a dull line of box-trees, where open succeeded open the livelong day of travel with wearisome iteration. By noon I had unconsciously almost drained my water-bag dry. It was with a sudden start, as though I woke in terror, that I found it nearly empty, and the anguish of thirst grew with maddening rapidity when I no longer dared to drink. My poor horse had been threatening to fall lame, and I could not urge her to a pace faster than a walk, and for ever as we went over the scorching ground the musical murmur of the little liquid still remaining in the bag grew more enticing and more tormenting. Had I known the country, or been more fortunate, I should have reached a station in the evening; but I came at last to two ways with such equal signs of travel, that there was no choice between them but that of chance, and of course I took the left and the wrong road. It led me to no house or water, but to a pile of cut wood only, and there I had to camp in the gathering darkness in such thirst that I took no thought of the food I carried with me. My horse was in such straits that I was obliged to tether her, or in her search for water I might never have seen her again. The night passed in wakefulness and anguish of no common order, for the thirst of even a few hours in a hot sun and dry atmosphere is far more dreadful and distressing than hunger, even when protracted for days.

At the very earliest dawn I rose dry-mouthed, saddled my horse, whose coat was already staring, and retraced our steps to the parting of the roads. By the time we reached it the level sun was flooding the silent and solitary plain with floods of misty light, tingeing the far belts of box with passing gold, and giving out even at that early hour sufficient heat to make me dread the time of noon. By eleven o'clock I passed the final belt of trees, and saw, just saw, the corrugated-iron roofs of the next station glittering in the sun at the far verge of the longest plain I had yet reached, one that was nearly fifteen miles across. I took my bag from the saddle, drank a few drops of water, and pouring the scant remainder into my hollowed hand, gave it to my horse, and then commenced the last stage of my journey. I can well remember how maddening it was to see the place to which I was journeying, and yet to know how far it was away; to know that there must be water there in abundance, and yet to be almost choking for a drink; to feel the sun increasing every moment in power, and to catch its reflected glare from the ground beneath me. What water I had taken but made me long for more, and indeed its effect was scarcely momentary, for my tongue grew parched and dry and stuck to my mouth, my lips cracked, and perspiration wholly ceased, though I was in the full rays of the sun. It took me three hours to cross that long last plain, and they were almost three eternities of torture, but when they were over the pleasure of drinking and of seeing my horse drink was more than I could have believed. I had often read of thirst, but now I can understand what it means, while to most it is but an unknown horror which they only as vaguely conceive as some mythologic monster that concerns them not.

And the next day at about nine in the morning I came to plentiful water—to the Big Billabong. And beyond it lay a true plain, without a tree, without a bit of scrub, a dull, long, dry, threatening level, running bare to the very horizon. I who had but just suffered from thirst pondered long as to whether I should venture into such a country. I knew that only a few miles beyond sight was the town of Urana. I had been told of it, but in my heart I refused to believe that any human beings could live there. It was like original exploration in a thirst land, and though I had planned going northward I could not bear to leave the cool and plentiful water and the shadow of the gums. I was fairly scared of that sun-burnt desert. That is why I changed my course and went south-south-east along the Billabong At any rate, food or none, I should not die of thirst. In the evening I reached Mahonga, owned by a man who is known all over Australia as "Bobby Rand." A little dry stick of a station-owner he was, but though he had no work for me I was at liberty to stay that night if I liked. On going to the kitchen I found a woman cooking there, and I had a very good meal, the first satisfactory one for several days. I was glad to hear that there was some chance of my obtaining a job from a man doing contract work for "Bobby," for my horse began to show signs of unsoundness which required no veterinary surgeon to recognize. In the morning, leaving her in the paddock, I put my blankets on my back, and with a mightily confused map of my seven-mile journey set out to find something to do. And very naturally I lost my way. To follow a chock and log fence for about a mile, then cross it and go at an angle till I struck a belt of timber, to go through that until I found a brush fence, and so on, landed me at last in a piece of scrub, not knowing in the least where anywhere might be.

However, knowing that I should come to another fence if I only kept in one direction, and that where a fence was a road must in the end be found, I set forward, and to my delight at last heard something which was distinctly made by men—the unmistakable sound of an axe. I came to some rail-splitters, who instantly knocked off work, glad of any excuse to "boil the billy" and drink some tea. How Australia would get on without that favourite drink is a puzzle to me. If, as the Colonials say, "stringy bark and raw hide" are the salvation of Australia, by giving them roofing material and something to tie things with, tea appears to be the support of the Australians themselves. So the splitters and I sat down and fraternized over the fragrant pannikin. I learnt that I was not very far out of my road, for Brown's camp was less than two miles away. By following an easily found fence I reached it an hour afterwards, and was hired at once to drive the horses and carts which took the earth from the great excavation, called a tank, in which the rainy season's water was to be caught. With Brown I remained at very hard work for seven weeks, rising at dawn, and labouring till dark.

It was now fast approaching summer, and the hottest part of it, and the heavens above were a cloudless and open blue. Our slight camp was situated in a small hollow, as we were naturally in a spot most advantageous for catching the rainwater, and round us on every side was dense forest or almost impassable scrub. The trees were the universal box, with a few soft-wooded currajongs, so regular in shape as to suggest Dutch gardening, and numberless varieties of bushes, some more nearly approaching weeds, and others only to be distinguished from trees by their size. Here also was to be found the quandong tree, the stones of which make such pretty necklaces. The ground, especially about our kitchen, was covered with countless swarms of ants, bull-dogs and sugar-ants, the small black venomous pismire, and hosts of unnamed others; there were large hairy tarantulas, or triantelopes, as we called them in the native language, which would have been barely extinguished by a saucer, and other spiders of strange and uncanny appearance and ferocious reputation. Under the rotting roots lay large centipedes, and beneath the rails made to fence the tank we every now and again found a fierce scorpion or brown snake. The trees about us were inhabited by iguanas of a size approaching that of small crocodiles, and the birds who scanned our proceedings in their ancient demesnes were bright and numerous. Among these the bell bird was very plentiful, and I heard its note every morning while hunting for the horses, and sometimes it led me astray. It is not like the famous campanero of the Brazilian forests, whose voice is as the sound of a hammer striking a large anvil, to be heard for miles, but it is light, airy, at times as faint as the far-distant ghost of a sound, like a bell of dreamland, or a single note remembered in after years. Those who listen to it cannot say "it is here," or "it is there"; they cannot with assurance affirm that there are many birds, or only one with a strange echoing gift of tongues. There is, I know not why, something pathetic in it, something curiously sweet, whether from its quality or suggestions, although it does not chime with a more recurrent and regular rhythm than the broken music of sounding streams. Perhaps it may be that it is so unearthly that we hear and dream in waking, being bidden to think of another world, that it is suggestive of something past and dead, or that it prophesies in melancholy something not yet to be. I have stayed in early morning in the quiet forest with the level sun staring at me through the windless trees, and listened with bent head and uplifted finger as though I suddenly heard a summons that was meant for me alone, as though I caught a sound that was inaudible by others, and as though I might, by an abstraction of thought from my visible surroundings, behold that invisible world which seems at such moments hidden but by a thin and impalpable veil.

In all tropical and sub-tropical climates there is a possibility of a sudden storm during the summer, and usually the more unexpected it is, the greater is its force and the more terrible the devastation that it works. It was well into December ere the work upon which I was employed reached its completion; and three days before we did the last strokes of our long task there came a storm of tropical intensity, which was startling both by its fury and short duration. The wind had been blowing softly all the morning from the north-west, and yet clouds, the first I had seen for months, were gradually gathering in the south-east. By noon all that quarter was black, half the heavens to the very zenith were hidden in murky obscurity, and as though it had been agreed upon by the powers of wind and rain that the clouds reaching so far should be the signal for devastation, the storm suddenly smote us, with no more warning than a few preliminary splashes of heavy rain. In one moment the wind blew a hurricane, and was almost solid—to walk against it was like going through water up to the chin; the dust rose up in one blinding mass, and was instantly smitten to the ground by rain which fell in sheets, and was torn into foam and smoke ere it touched the earth; sticks and branches hurtled through the air; the leaves were stripped from the bent trees, and went level in the screaming wind like a solid flight of green parroquets; and even in the most sheltered forest tree after tree came down with a crash—some torn up by the roots, and others, solid and sound though they might be, were smashed and splintered and their whole crowns thrown yards from the shattered stumps. Our tents lay flat or bellying upon the ground, even though we were camped behind the dam we had raised; the slight structure which had been our kitchen suddenly disappeared, while pots and pans and pannikins rattled and bowled along the ground, as we lay down praying that none of the flying branches might fall upon us. And the rain fell in floods, and in no floods of a figure of speech. This pandemonium lasted just one quarter of an hour, and then, as suddenly as it

had begun, so suddenly it ceased; the black clouds flew past us, the sun shone out hotly in a clear sky, and save for the mud, the disordered camp, and our great tank more than three-quarters full, there was no sign of the squall which had made us fear for our lives, and had taught us what a tornado was and what it could do. But it made the grass grow green again for a few days, the grass that would be so surely needed ere the summer was past, for it was getting towards Christmas, and the thermometer stood higher and higher every day.

That summer job of mine was surely very hard work. I was called the horse-driver, and drive I did, but I learnt to use the pick and shovel as well during that hot seven weeks. The axe, then an almost unknown implement to me, took a great deal of learning Dora Dora only taught me that it was a difficult thing to handle, but the camp in Morgan's paddock made me fairly proficient.

The hole in the ground which we called the tank, and from which I helped to take the last five thousand cubic yards of "dirt" (in all it measured fifteen thousand) was surrounded by a fence. I dug many of the post holes with spade and bar. The posts were bored for wire. I bored them in the intervals of driving, just as a recreation. The way left open to the water was corduroyed with small trees pegged down to large ones sunk lengthways on the slope. With a great two-inch auger I made the peg holes. Occasionally I made mortice holes. Now, as every worker knows, every tool makes its natural blisters on a soft hand. The axe raises them in one place, the saw in another, the bar in a third. The auger selects the middle of the palm. As I took up new tools one after the other, blister after blister rose, until at one time on both hands I could count forty places were they were or had been, to say nothing of others quite healed and passed out of sight under new and hardened epithelium. As I was always dabbling in water, or handling wet clay, my skin never got a rest, the tender new skin cracked, my hands were covered with blood; every tool I touched I left a mark on. The pain and agony were often exquisite, I wonder now that I did not throw up my job and go off on the "wallaby track" once more. But there is at times a certain unthinking tenacity about me. I worked doggedly on day by day, determined to stay till the job was finished. There were no compensations. Our only amusement was throwing sticks at the gigantic iguanas who frequented the trees about the camp. They were often over six feet in length, and one we particularly noticed was nearly nine; a kind of arboreal crocodile he seemed. On Sundays, I sometimes wandered into the thick scrub of the paddock and gathered quandongs, taking out the stones. As fruit, the quandong is not a success.

As I said above, the paddock in which we worked was known as Morgan's paddock, being named after the most celebrated Australian bushranger. It had been in the old days one of his favourite hiding-places, for the thickness and impenetrability of the scrub made it comparatively safe. Like the tiger that he sometimes was, he lurked in the jungle. At times, when quite alone in the scrub, a mile from our camp, I used to think of Morgan, the solitary criminal, with no friend, no companion but his horse, sitting there too, never quite safe for a moment, never at peace, never able to sleep in quiet, for ever with his hands upon the weapons with which he was such a dead shot. Bobby Rand and he knew each other very well; and on more than one occasion the squatter had to furnish the outlaw with a horse. None but the best suited Morgan. It was a case of *force majeure.* Some months after I left Mahonga I travelled with a man who worked on that station when Morgan was in the neighbourhood. He came in one evening when work was over, ordered every one into the kitchen except the overseer, whom he set playing in the house on a kind of harmonium, with orders to keep on at music under pain of death. Rand himself and his men sat in the kitchen while Morgan had supper, with his revolvers on the table. His hard and awful life was beginning to tell on him. His face was pallid and worn, the eyes burning as in a kind of delirium; he was restless and nervous. Yet even so he was able to ride a young horse which bucked very hard. That was next morning. He sat the buck-jumper like a born horseman, and, as I was told, held the reins in his teeth, keeping his six-shooters in his hands, never for a moment taking his eyes from the crowd. He feared being shot from behind, as he afterwards was at Pidgiebar in Victoria.

It is a curious example of the fact that Morgan for all his occasional bloodthirstiness was not altogether a bad man, that he took a real interest in the working men's wages and food. Not infrequently they growled to him of the inadequacy of their allowance of provisions. He would have a talk with their employer on the subject. It may easily be imagined that his slightest suggestions were attended to at once. Like the American who chased another for two miles with an axe, " he warn't a man to go projeckin' with." Of course there is a sad quantity of myth grown up about the man, as there is about every bushranger, and it is often difficult to disentangle the truth from the falsehood. These outlaws are a stock subject for conversation round the camp fire, and share with horses, gold mining, and ribaldry the talk of the evening after work.

When it was evident that we should put the final touches to the tank in about a week, I began to think of getting some other employment. While reading a newspaper published at Albury, I noticed an advertisement by a man not three miles from our camp. He wanted a tutor for his three children. The next Sunday I walked through the bush to his place, and offered my services in that capacity. I was a rough enough looking tutor, but as I had a certificate of matriculation at London University in my pocket-book, I proffered that as a testimonial to my education. It had as much effect as if it had been a voucher of a double first at Oxford, and it was with evident regret that he owned to having already hired some one who had been beforehand with me. Still, if I wanted work, he would give it me on the completion of the tank. I was to do odd jobs—in fact, be a general rouseabout—for a pound a week and my grub. Having settled that, I went back to the camp. In three days we had cleared up everything. I took my money, bade farewell to my mates, and walked over to take up my duties in a new situation.

CHAPTER VI.

THE GREAT HEAT.

My new employer was by no means a man of the same character as Brown, the contractor I had just left. There was no ruthless energy about him, and he was well satisfied if I did a moderately fair amount of work. This suited my temperament, for though I can work hard enough at times, I entirely disbelieve in it except as a *pis aller*. Labour was and is and will be a curse, until each man does his own, in his own way, at his own time. To some extent I had my own way on this little station. There were not many sheep, perhaps only some five thousand; we had a few cows, but at this period of my life I could not milk, and they were attended to by Annie, a big, robust, and kindly Australian girl, who was the cook. She and I got on very well together, and never quarrelled very violently. At most stations a man has to wash his own clothes, and rough washing they got from me, as I objected to that Sunday's job, but here Annie did them for me. I cut the wood for the kitchen, did some clearing in the home paddock, ringed a few score trees, killed a sheep every now and again, and occasionally mended a fence. But in my second week there, I had to knock off work and lay up with a bad hand. An unaccustomed axeman sometimes jars his hand when felling timber, and the jar results very often in a kind of whitlow, or rather perhaps a touch of periostitis. My right forefinger got very bad; it was impossible to use it. Presently, after a day or two of idleness, the suffering became intense. Neither by day nor night could I rest. All night long I walked in the moonlight between the house and the little shanty in which my bed was; I threw myself down in exhaustion; and rose again to resume my monotonous tramp. For four days and nights I did not sleep. The boss's wife and Annie were very kind to me, but in spite of all they could do, I came very near performing a sudden and ruthless operation on my finger with a sharp tomahawk. Had it been any other than the trigger finger, I think I should have parted with it. But on the fifth day a deep incision with a knife brought me relief. I soon recovered, and went to work again. Yet in the growing heat I remained languid for some time.

The greenness resulting from that fierce rain while I was at the tank lasted but a few days, and the summer sun soon reduced everything save the stubborn box-trees to a universal brown. The paths and roads about us were almost axle-deep in dust, and the sandhills were like dry quicksand, threatening to engulf the labouring teams. The air for the most part was calm and still, but when it blew, the clouds of dust and sand nearly choked man and beast; while here and there on the windless days fantastic whirlwinds that were vast and funnel-shaped stalked across the plain, revolving with terrific rapidity and loud hissing, which when seen against the sun first turned the blazing orb dun red, and then hid it for a moment and passed away into the distance. The air was hot and heavy, burning the throat and lungs and drying up the skin; the rays of the sun came back redoubled from the fiery ground, whose heat could be felt through the sole of a man's boot, and the earth was weary and panted, while the bitter and cloudless blue above was pitiless and implacable.

It seemed impossible that the heat could increase, and yet as Christmas drew near it grew hotter and hotter still; and though every day we declined, almost in terror, to believe that the thermometer could get any higher, still every day it was some degrees above what it had been upon the yesterday On Christmas Day it was 115° in the shade, four days afterwards 120°, and on the first of the new year it stood at 125°, and did not alter for three days. This was in the shade under a verandah, but what it was in the sun I did not have the courage to inquire or the capacity to calculate. The sky was intensely blue, with a whitish haze near the horizon, and the wind now blew steadily from the tropics; a north wind that slowly passed over nearly two thousand miles of burning plains as it moved to the south, gathering warmth as it came, until it was like the blast of heat that comes from a tapped furnace when the molten metal runs in dazzling whiteness. The sheep and horses stood all day in the shade, with their drooping heads towards the tree-trunks; the fowls kept in shelter as well, and, like the quadrupeds, they too panted with open mouths and lolling tongues. The ground in the sun was as hot as fire, hardly to be touched with the hand, nor at midnight was there any perceptible alteration or remission, for even then metal was almost too hot to take hold of. Water left out in the sun for a few hours disappeared almost as if it had been boiling, and we were all in a state of perspiration that was weakening to an extreme degree. Birds even were found dead, struck by the sun in their flight, and there was a sombre melancholy about everything; it looked indeed as if all nature were ready to die, for hope seemed lost and strength exhausted.

After the slow passing of those three long days the thermometer went down with an exasperating deliberation, first to 120°, where it halted for a while, and then to 115°, at which point it remained until nearly the end of January, when it dropppd quickly to 100°, which seemed pleasantly cool to us and quite reasonable.

Soon after Christmas, as there was very little to do at the station, my employer "lent" me, so to speak, to a man with a contract to split rails. This was quite agreeable to me, and I went to work with the axe felling colonial pine. This is a pretty enough tree to look at, and makes fairly good rails, although it is not very enduring, but as sawed timber it is the poorest in the world. To put a nail into an inch board without first boring a hole would split it from end to end. But it was easy stuff to cut, and I threw them down one after another in

the early dawn, often working by myself from four o'clock till six before the boss came. It was by far the pleasantest time in the day, there was even a kind of freshness in the air, and the quiet bush a mile from any habitation was absolutely peaceful. As each tree fell with a crash into the scrub I sat down and took a smoke. My water-bag hung on a swaying branch near by. I was fairly happy in those morning hours. When there were two of us we got the cross-cut saw to work, sawed the trees into lengths, and split them with mauls and wedges. I found the pine child's play after box and red gum. By nine o'clock we finished work and went to the tin hut where my temporary boss lived with his wife. We had a slight meal, for it was difficult to eat much in that hot weather, and lying down on the floor on stretched blankets we took a long siesta, often remaining there till three or four. That long noon was painful, it was so impossible to rest, both on account of the intense heat and the hideous Australian plague of flies. For these choke the air, they buzz, and hum and hunt you, they are a summer torture, a long, bitterly persisting onset; they are unresting, incapable of fatigue, hungry, esurient; they enter your mouth, your ears, you catch them in your eyelids; they thirst for the moisture of your lips; they render life intolerable, and Australia a nightmare. Mosquitoes are bad, their sting is painful, the after itching cruel, but they are rare save by water, near creeks or swamps, or after rain; but these flies are ubiquitous, and the daylight hears them humming hungrily for ever over all the long plains of the continent south of Capricorn. And then the ants rejoiced in the fiery heat and grew active—sugar-ants, and the fierce small pismire, and the inch long bull-dog whose bite is like the stab of a red-hot lancet. Spiders crawled and swung everywhere— tarantulas, the black spider with the red triangle sacred to Bass's beer on his back, great hairy spiders long legged and diabolical and rough. And scorpions lay under logs, and on disturbance flourished the lithe deadly pointed long jointed tail; centipedes brown and black crawled about slowly, some small, others half a foot long that one loathed to crush and yet destroyed. For Australia is the great land of the Fly and the Insect: a happy hunting-ground for entomologists. At Mahonga the ophiologist would have deserted his specialty; in three months I only killed two snakes, one a brilliant brown backed opalescent white bellied active devil, and black one. Dora Dora in the late spring was the place for them, for snakes love water, and by the Murray they flourish. I killed a black snake six feet four inches long as I walked to Albury: in the bush I rode over them, they rustled thick in the riverside grass.

This rail splitting work lasted nearly three weeks, and then I went back to my old place, where I was very lazy without hearing any remonstrances from my easy-going employer. As I piled up fallen branches and sticks in the paddock he often came to see me, and we chatted for an hour as we sat on a log. All this time I have said nothing of the tutor whose job I had applied for. Yet he was a man deserving at least a notice. In age about fifty, he was in strength a man of thirty, and very powerful for that. Six feet high, and some forty-five round the chest, he walked as upright as a pine. He was, or had been, or might have been, something like a gentleman. His appearance was not altogether such as inspires confidence, though he was very handsome; there was an uneasiness about him at one time and a recklessness at another which was curious. English of course, but he had been in the colonies for years. I came to the conclusion that he had left England for some good reason. We often talked together, but he never told me anything about himself. I know that the man who employed us both felt as I did about him. He was sorry he had ever hired him. Yet he did his work well enough, and taught the three young children quite as much as they would learn: at the same time building a kind of schoolroom, for he was a very good carpenter. Sometimes he wrote articles for the paper published at Piney Ridge, some twenty miles west of Mahonga, and these were very well done. Altogether he was an interesting man. I have never been able to quite fathom the reasons for my almost fearing him. Yet sometimes I think I know.

At the end of twelve weeks after my leaving Brown's Camp it became quite evident to me that there was so little to do that I was not needed to do it. The same obvious fact dawned at last on the boss, and with many apologies he wrote me a cheque and dismissed me. I left the station in the company of a man who was taking a bullock waggon loaded with wool down to Albury. We were two days and a half on the journey, camping twice on the way down. During the last day we were rather short of water and I got a morbid and insatiable thirst on me. As we neared the town we came to a tank or dam, where the water was hot in the blazing sun. I was choked with dust, and drank until I nearly burst. Three miles further we reached a grog shanty; I swallowed two bottles of soda-water. On the outskirts of the town I went to a house and asked for something to drink, and took almost a quart of water. In a few minutes more I was in town. The road led by the back of the vicarage where Roland had gone when we came up from Melbourne. I thought I would call, just as I was, without going to the

hotel; but I went in the back way. The servant stared at me, as well she might. I had my blankets on my back like any ordinary "traveller," my clothes were ragged, my complexion the colour of a coffee berry. And of course I was covered with dust. I asked for the clergyman's sister, as I knew her better than the others. She came out, and when she recognized me asked me in, laughing good-humouredly at my extraordinary roughness. I only stayed a few minutes, much to the relief of the servant, who failed to grasp the situation, and evidently did not like "travellers."

CHAPTER VII.

CARABOBLA AND YARRA YARRA.

My tramping into Albury had been in consequence of having no horse. The mare that carried me to Bobby Rand's I sold for a couple of pounds to Brown at the tank, being glad enough to get rid of her at such a price; for I now began to know a little about horses, and their soundness or unsoundness. At my last place of work there had been several young colts and fillies. There is no easier way to learn a little about outside common veterinary knowledge than to get well acquainted with the shape and feel of the legs of youngsters not yet knocked about and spoiled or rendered unsound. So when I came back to Albury for the last time, I felt more able to buy a horse without being greatly cheated. But I had a few days to spend with Roland before going off into the bush again, and for a little while I became almost civilized.

Yet it was very curious to sleep in a good bed again. At Mahonga and in Morgan's paddock my couch was nothing but a sheet of stringy bark, stripped from the tree, flattened out and left to dry until it grew as hard as a board. On this I put my blankets; my pillow was my coat and any odd clothes or rags of clothes that I might have. I grew used to this primitive fashion of sleeping: the hardness of the bark did not trouble me. I found it as difficult to get up as if I had been lapped in luxury. In fact what would seem egregious discomfort to most became luxury to me, and when I turned into a bed with sheets and pillows and all civilized appurtenances I could not sleep at all. I rolled and tumbled and tossed and growled, but rest would not come. I felt choked in a room, preferring the open air, or a draughty tent, or a shanty which was only an apology for a shelter. At last in desperation I rose, set the windows wide open, put a chair to the door to prevent it closing, dragged the blankets off the bed and slept soundly on the floor. The chambermaid found me thus in the morning, and laughed at my hatred of a bed. Before I got used to sheets and soft mattresses I was away from town again. I had become something of a savage.

The heat which we had experienced at Mahonga was of course almost universal in New South Wales, and in consequence grass was a memory and a hope rather than a thing existing. With the failure of pasturage, horses get cheap; it is better to sell animals at a low price than to see them die of hunger and thirst. So one day there was a sale of horses in the town stockyard. I went down there thinking it probable I might pick up one at a reasonable price. There were about sixty in the yard, horses, mares, fillies and colts; some good, some poor, some big and big boned, others weedy and of little promise. It was a burning hot day, and the horses as they were rushed here and there to part one for sale, raised a choking cloud of dust. Most of us sat on the fences; all the lazy young boys of the town were there to watch. Prices ruled very low even for that time. Horse after horse sold for one pound, then two, perhaps three. One very fine iron grey, broken to saddle and harness, and sixteen hands high, fetched the top price, selling for as much as nine pounds. At last I saw one I thought would suit me, a bright bay standing an inch over fifteen hands, rising five years. Some one bid ten shillings, another a pound, then another went to thirty. As this last man was a very good judge of horses, he encouraged me to bid two pounds. The bidding was very slack, but at last it rose to three pounds fifteen, increasing then by half-crowns until my very good horse Devilskin passed to me for four pounds seven and sixpence. After that the other horses went quickly and for nothing. The auctioneer could get no bid for one weedy yearling until he turned to the boys with "Come boys, now's your chance." A little lad about seven bid sixpence. It was knocked down to another child for four and sixpence. One boy bought a colt for six shillings. Prices were certainly not high, and a man remarked that it reminded him of the Parkes "penny mob" of horses, where it took a first class horse to cost a sovereign. I never regretted my purchase, although the name I gave him was bestowed after some experience. He threw me the second time I rode him, and nearly broke my neck. He had a delightfully neat trick of "propping" or halting suddenly without any provocation. But he never got rid of me after I learned his little ways, and I forgave his faults when I found he had good paces and great endurance. He was to carry me from Albury to the Willandra Billabong, from the land of the eucalyptus to the great salt-bush plains. The third day after the sale I left Albury. It occurred to me that I might go up to Dora Dora again, and riding through Bowna, I reached it at noon the second day. After a chat with Mr. T—— who showed me the ravages a fire had caused on the lower ranges, making them as bare of foliage as the flats of Thologolong across the Murray, I rode through the Tunnel, and called at Mitchell's. Thence I travelled to Gerogery and Ten Mile Creek, a little straggling township. My objective was Carabobla.

While working in Albury as the stock and station agent's clerk, I had made the acquaintance of a Mrs. M——, the daughter of a doctor, well known in that part of the Riverina. I also knew another of his daughters. Mrs. M—— had been kind enough to ask me to call if I ever came that way. She was a widow living on her own property near her father's station. As I was very near Carabobla at Ten Mile Creek, I turned my horse's head north, and left the main road. After a three or four mile ride, I came to a little house with a garden in front. I tied my horse to the fence and went in to inquire the way to Mrs. M——. She herself came to the door. After giving me a cup of tea in a civilized manner, not out of a billy as I was now accustomed to take it, I caught and saddled her horse and we rode together through the bush to her father's house. They asked me to stay for a week, for the hospitality of New South Wales is always as free as sunlight in a land of the sun. I was nothing loth to turn my horse loose, and sit under a rose-covered verandah by a garden which ran to the edge of the Great Billabong, at that season quite dry. The Doctor's youngest son Will became my chum at once; in the company of pleasant and natural people, young girls and men, with a charming hostess and a kind host, I was as happy as running water, as bright as dawn. For once in Australia I did nothing but amuse myself with a free mind. As it was then long after shearing, Will had little to do; we rode about the country; sometimes I lent him a hand at fence mending; for recreation with a spice of danger in it we went honey hunting.

The wild bee in Australia is the *Apis mellifica* of Europe and the whole civilized world, and as in America, it has spread over a great part of the continent. On the Murray river and in the whole of the Riverina, where it is not for ever dry, and there are numbers of flowers, it is especially plentiful. Though it may seem a mild enough pursuit, in my opinion it is the only dangerous game to go for in all the ancient land of the marsupials. One has to exercise a considerable amount of awkwardness, and to display much native stupidity to get hurt by a kangaroo; the innocent native bear is no more a bear than it is a shark; the sneaking dingo when run down on horseback will turn over to be killed; and as for the fierce and formidable mosquito, man is his prey rather than the reverse. The first time I ever went honey hunting was at Dora Dora, where Bill Stewart, the man who owned Flo, the celebrated sheep dog, inveigled me into the bush. It took some persuasion to induce me to brave bees in their native wilds, for I distinctly remember having as a child played the fool with a beehive, a course of proceeding which naturally resulted in hartshorn and the blue-bag. I argued that if such were the case with the tame, domestic, civilized bee, the wild ones would be infinitely worse. However, after a judiciously applied series of taunts, Bill induced me to shoulder the axe and take a bucket in hand, though I own that I would much rather have mounted a buck-jumper of the worst description. It seemed better to die of a broken neck than to be stung to death.

The knowledge I possessed of the bush at that

time was just sufficient to enable me to get lost on the very shortest notice, and it seemed to me that Stewart was cruelly reckless both of his own life and mine when he plunged into the thick forest and proceeded to climb an almost inaccessible hill. By the time the sharp stubs of wattles had nearly torn my shirt off my back, I was utterly exhausted. But presently we stayed under a big gum tree, perched on a slope as steep as the roof of a house, and my mate informed me that it was a bee tree. He tried to persuade me that he had known of it before; but I scorned his assurances, not being able to believe that any man could find one particular tree in such a forest. However, we commenced cutting it down. It was the first time I ever handled an axe seriously, and the amount of physical strength I expended in making an ugly, irregular gash in the bark would have sufficed an American from the forests of Michigan for a week's work. Stewart smiled grimly, and set me aside. In about an hour it was evident the tree would soon fall, and desiring to do something serious I took up the axe again.

I had noticed a bee come down every now and again as if to inspect our proceedings, but as none of them attempted to attack me my confidence returned. I began to scorn the wild Australian bee, believing that its native ferocity had been undermined by the mild climate of its adopted country. But the tree began to shake, and a bee, evidently much disturbed in mind, flew down fiercely. It made three rapid circles round the trunk, and then, satisfied that I was undermining the constitution of the state, flew right in my face, and stung me under the eye. I dropped the axe with a loud yell, and went uphill like a kangaroo. As I started the tree gave a crack and yielded. It fell with a terrible crash almost on its crown, and the bees came out in a wild excited crowd. I cannot understand why others did not attack us, but we cut the honey out of their hollow branch without more than three stings each. My face did not swell, but Stewart's right eye closed, and the left one nearly disappeared with it. If he had been rendered quite blind we should have been obliged to remain until next day, for I could not have found my way home. It took me months to acquire, even in a primitive way, some kind of instinct of self-guidance.

The honey that we found was of very fair quality, though it ran all shades of colour, from the white new comb to the deeply stained remains of past years, and the acacia or wattle blossoms give it a pleasant aromatic odour.

This day's experience at Dora Dora and my comparatively easy escape, made me readier than I should have been to go out with Will and fell the trees which his keen eyes had marked as having bees in them. As he rode about the paddocks, with the true instinct of a colonial boy he could remember each hive, and sometimes he added the knowledge of another. Not having cut down any for some time, till I came, he had quite a farm of bees ready for the axe. The pursuit was, it is true, sometimes like gambling. One day we determined to cut down a tree about three feet six inches in diameter, and being firmly convinced that there was much honey in the great hollow limb sixty feet above us, we took a small hand-sledge with a great tin tub on it instead of a bucket. We cut away for a couple of hours, and then took a rest, for the wood was solid and hard, and we were young, or at least I was, at the axe. After another half hour's hot toil, the mighty tree came down with a crash. We took no more than a quart of honey from the hollow branch. Evidently the bees had only lately taken up their abode in it; perhaps they had been dispossessed from some ancient hive but a week or two before. In silent disgust we threw the light comb into the tub, and started to look for another tree. Presently we came to one about sixteen inches in diameter. Was it worth cutting down, we asked each other? In so small a trunk could there be much honey? "At any rate," I said, hitting the bark with the back of my axe, "it is half rotten, and won't take ten minutes to bring down. So here goes!" Out of that thin box-tree we took enough honey to almost fill the tub. The comb filled the whole hollow trunk for a space of nearly three feet, and as the thin shell burst with the fall, the honey oozed out everywhere. At the top it was pure white, growing yellow and then brown, and almost black, as the comb of past years came in sight. But it was all good. At the house there was a busy time straining it and making mead. That lucky find set us free for other amusements: the supply would last for months.

I have never seen practised in Australia any of the elaborate scientific methods which are employed in America to discover the home of the bees. "Angling" is unknown, and no one makes a profession or business of honey hunting. But as a recreation in the late summer it is pleasant, and often exciting. To stand on the fallen trunk and cut out the comb while a thousand bees are flying round one's head in a thick cloud, gives a sensation of daring adventure not often afforded by "bailing up" a wretched kangaroo in a country which is singularly and universally devoid of those animals which satisfy the love of danger in hunting on the western prairies or Rocky Mountains of North America. If any one

thinks this is not so, he can easily remove his doubts by upsetting a hive in the neighbouring garden, previously making a firm resolution that he will not run away.

I never noticed the small black stingless bee of Australia; but my brother Cecil, who worked for a long time in Queensland, says it is very common there. It does not make a true comb, and the honey is very thin and watery. The natives call it a name equivalent to "sugar bag," and are very fond of it.

After remaining in this pastoral home by the Billabong for a week I ran up my horse from the paddock, put the saddle on him, and began to make up my swag. But my hostess would not allow me to go; some other visitors were coming in a day or two, it was proposed to give a small party. Would I remain? I fancied I saw myself going away under those circumstances—going away into the wan and desolate bush to ride in solitude through scrub and over long dusty plains, to suffer from thirst and perhaps hunger, while here was ready and instant hospitality. My "no" had little more than the hesitation which extorts a repeated request. I loosed Devilskin and unrolled my blankets. The next day was a Sunday, and we rode into Ten Mile Creek to listen to the only sermon I heard in New South Wales, save of course in Albury, where I was bound more or less to listen to what my friend Roland's clergyman said to us weekly. The church ride would have been pleasant enough—there were four girls on horseback, Will and I—but my mount showed strong atheistic principles, refusing to go to church except on violent persuasion, which led to buck-jumping that nearly unseated me. When it seemed that the conflict would last long enough to make them late the others left me, "still sitting" happily, for Devilskin could not get me off. About a quarter of an hour's further struggle made him give in, and going at a good gallop I caught up our party two miles from Ten Mile Creek. The chapel looked curious enough. It was surrounded by buggies or carriages of all descriptions; to each carriage a horse, or a pair, was attached; every fence was crowded with saddle horses. In all there were some hundred animals there to occasionally break the monotonous service by an angry squeal or a kick. When service was over we thought we had done our duty. With the exception of the trouble with my dissentient or dissenting horse, our ride there had been sober enough, but going back we went across country at a gallop, taking all the brush fences in our way. For the New South Wales girls can ride like feminine centaurs. We came back with our horses foaming, and got very properly chided by the elder people for our unseemly behaviour.

The little party came off the next day and was a great success; many girls and young men came from the neighbouring stations; we danced till a late hour, and varied dancing by walking about in the brilliant moonlight. As the house was quite full, Will and I and some other youngsters slept in tents set up the day before near the Billabong. Next day we escorted some of the ladies home. It was about the only time I ever did anything so civilized in the bush; it was the only place I ever stayed at in Australia as a friend. In others I was a traveller, a "sundowner," a "swagsman," or a "hand" of some description.

Three or four days later on my host's recommendation I went seventeen miles across the ranges and asked for work at Yarra Yarra. This I got at once, and began by looking after the fences in a gang which was nicknamed the Flying Squadron, a kind of collection of boundary riders. Yarra Yarra was a sheep-station, but the one thing I noticed there particularly was the number of dogs. Every man on the place, and there were many, seemed to own one or two. There were scores no one owned. The squatter himself had a few fine kangaroo dogs, which are like very large and heavy greyhounds; there were sheep-dogs, retrievers, mongrels of every description. At night time the ground about the house was black with them; it required in favourite spots care to avoid treading on them; if anything happened there was an unmelodious howling which raised the station. And by day they foraged and fought and played and courted until Yarra Yarra in my memory seems like one gigantic kennel. But I did not stay there long. The very next Sunday after my arrival I got my horse and rode over to Carabobla. Devilskin strained himself on the range by treading on a loose stone, and I was unable to get back that night. When I reached Yarra Yarra in the morning I was a little later than the usual working hour and very promptly was given the sack. I went back the same day to Carabobla, stayed there that night, and in the morning started on a northward journey which lasted three months and landed me on the other side of the Lachlan river.

CHAPTER VIII.

A THREE MONTHS' RIDE.

IT was late in the summer when I finally left Carabobla; the grass was scanty, the water-holes half empty. Here and there, indeed, they were only plashy mud, whence the sheep sucked what moisture they could before it was trodden into a thick mass which mired the weaker ones and held them till help or death came. The roads were dusty; dust lay thick upon the trees, and yet in the air was a feeling that Nature was going to help man and beast with a little rain. The second day of my northward travel brought a heavy shower, and for a week it rained a little every day. Each station I passed I asked for work, but work was none. My cash was very low; I had indeed but seventeen and sixpence on that second day. But I was on an unfrequented road; I already knew better than to take the Wagga Wagga track: that was sure to be well travelled, and instead of a meal with the men for nothing, liberty to put my horse in the paddock and my blankets in any spare bunk of the hut, I should have been obliged to take the pannikin of flour, the pinch of tea and sugar which constitutes a traveller's rations, to which minimum he thinks he has an inalienable right. We used to argue it out to ourselves in this way: "A squatter wants men, and often has a difficulty in getting them. If he wrote down to town he would have to wait, and, moreover, have to pay the expenses of the man who selected them, and their travelling expenses, running, moreover, the risk of having some sent up that he didn't like. So as we (the party arguing the question under a gum tree) come to his very door, the least he can do is to feed us." That is how we looked at it; but sometimes when twenty or thirty came in an evening, the squatter had doubts as he saw his diminishing sack of flour.

But on my road past Wallendool, Urangaline Creek, Brookong, and Boree Creek I had no trouble in getting all I wanted to eat without any question of paying. The only money I dispensed was two shillings for a water-bag. My other one was worn out and would hold nothing. But at Spring Creek I came across a traveller who possessed a very good one, and as he had no tobacco, and was accordingly extremely miserable, he parted with the bag. I filled it and went my way rejoicing, and having given him part of a fig of very strong tobacco, I left him sitting on his blankets blowing a cloud, which was a fair sign of content on his part.

Then I passed the long Buckenbong Lagoon through a comparatively good grass land. Jenkins of Buckenbong was as well known to all who travelled New South Wales as Bobby Rand of Mahonga, or Hungry Tyson, so called because he would never feed travellers, or Jacky Dow, of Toganmain, on whom all bush jokes are fathered, as we put bulls on the Irishman. I came suddenly to the Murrumbidgee and the Buckenbong home station. The river ran, as the Australian rivers of the plains do, in a deep channel. There was no great current; the banks were thick with gums. As there was no bridge within any reasonable distance, for Narrandera was miles west of me and Wagga Wagga far to the east, it was manifest I should have to swim it. However, a pleasant-looking woman came out on the verandah as I stayed to survey things, and in answer to my inquiries as to how I was to cross, she ordered three young black fellows, the aboriginal Australians, to row me over in a boat. So I put my saddle in and led Devilskin behind. It required the persuasive touch of a stockwhip, skilfully wielded by

a fourth black boy, to induce him to enter the water, but once in, he swam so fast that I had to let him go. I caught him easily on the farther bank, and, bestowing sixpence on the youngsters, rode on.

If there had been no one there to help me I should have had to swim across by myself. The crossing of rivers is often a ticklish business and requires a good deal of consideration, it being perfectly easy to drown one's horse and one's self too. For one thing, it is always necessary to unbuckle the reins, for if the horse gets nervous and pulls away from a boat, or if one is on his back and gets put off, the animal may thrust his foreleg through them and drown himself. One may ride the horse, or swim alongside holding his mane, or hang on by his tail. If he naturally swims very deep, it is best not to be on his back. But more accidents occur through the rider going in at the wrong place. It is often better to choose a comparatively bad place to go in if the landing places are few. When a stream is hedged about with dead timber the horse often plunges as soon as he touches bottom, and may stake himself. A little thought, a good survey of the river, and a careful calculation of the rate of the stream will usually put a man and his horse across any ordinary river in safety.

After leaving the river I came, about a mile further on, to a wire fence. The gate was very high and strong, and moreover locked. I had no wish to try to jump it, having never taken Devilskin over high timber, but at first there seemed no choice. However, I knew that there must be some way out. Men on horseback must often go that way. So I tied up my horse and hunted along the fence very carefully. Presently I chuckled with pride at my insight. One post had been carefully cut away at the top, so that part of it would pull out, leaving the upper wire free. I pulled out the chock, took the wire out of the slit, and bringing up Devilskin, took a stirrup leather from the saddle and carefully strapped the three wires together. I had now a very low jump, and on it I put my coat to show the horse plainly where the wire was. Mounting, I went back a few yards and rode over it easily. I put things as I found them and went on.

My object, if, indeed, I had one, in coming up this way through Urangaline, Brookong, and Buckenbong, was to get to a place called Grong Grong, on the northern side of Murrumbidgee. Mrs. M——'s brother-in-law had a new station there, and when I met him at Carabobla, where he stayed for a day in coming from Albury, he asked me to come to Grong Grong if I was ever that way. Until I reached Boree Creek I had hardly thought of this invitation, but the boree trees, of which I there saw a few, reminded me that his station was in the boree country. So I determined to go there. And now I could not be very far from the place. But whether it was to the right or left or straight ahead I could not tell. I found a road, or an apology for one, and followed it, and at sundown I came to a house.

"Is this Mr. M——'s?" I asked of a man sitting under the verandah. His answer almost paralyzed me.

"What do you want with Mr. M——?"

I stared at him for almost a minute, and then replied by another question.

"And why do you want to know what I want with him? Who are you any way?"

He started and looked angry.

"I know M——'s business as well as I know my own, and——"

I cut him short, thinking him either impertinent or crazy.

"If you do, this is my business. Have you any objection to my camping here?"

"Yes, I have. I don't like any one camping about my place."

Such a thing had never happened before in my short Australian experience, nor did I think it possible. I pointed out to him that it was rapidly growing dark, that I was in a wilderness of a country totally unknown to me, and that the customs of New South Wales were being most grossly outraged by him. He became quite sullen, and only growled when I said I wanted no food of him.

"Very well," I said at last, "perhaps you will tell me how to reach Grong Grong?"

"That's the road," he grunted, pointing down the fence towards the west.

"And is it easy?"

"Perfectly easy."

"Now," said I, "as you have been so kind to me, perhaps you will let me have a drink of water?"

And getting off my horse I went to a small tank and took some.

"Good-bye," said I, as I rode away; "I shall acquaint your neighbour, Mr. M——, with your genial courtesy."

I should have enjoyed breaking his head, and banging him against his own verandah posts. I don't believe there are half a dozen men in New South Wales capable of acting as he did. America is thick with such, but in Australia I so rarely met any unkindness of word or deed, that I boiled with rage as I went off into the gathering darkness. My gentle friend's perfectly plain path might have been plain to one who rode it every day; with light I might have found it, but the starlight is a poor path-finder. After following the fence for about two miles I got into dense scrub. Retracing my steps I found the track again, but lost it finally in what I found, on striking a match, to be sheep-trails. I used some strong language, which echoed in the forest, for here there were many trees, and now sought some open place to camp in. In a few minutes I came to an old sheep yard. I could go no further. But I dare not let my horse go. It was practically an unfenced country, the paddocks must be ten miles across, and I might lose him for days, even if I ever got him again. So taking off his saddle, I tied him to a post inside the yard. Finding a fairly soft place, I lay down in my blankets and tried to sleep. But sleep would not come. Thirst came instead, and because I had neglected in my anger to fill my water-bag I had nothing to drink. I began to get worried and feverish. Suddenly I felt a sharp sting like that of the fierce little black pismire ant. I rubbed the place and probably killed that explorer, but others followed, until I jumped up in anguish. A match showed that I had lain down on a nest of them. I had to strip to the skin to get clear of them. I shook my blankets and sought another place. Again the ants attacked me. Only on the third attempt did I succeed in finding a spot free of these poisonous little black devils. Then to irritate me by suggesting possibilities I heard a frog croak — a wretched, solitary frog. "There must be water somewhere," I said; but I could not find it. It was impossible to locate the sound. I lay down dry-mouthed, determined to sleep, if only a good try would bring me oblivion. Then a more-pork, the Australian night-jar, began in the biggest tree above me. He said in a melancholy way, with long drawn out insistence on the greedy syllables, "more-pork." In the distance came the answer, faint and far, from another of his race, "more-pork;" and this was repeated and again repeated, until I longed for a gun to make the wretched bird cease his foolish request. It is curious how absolutely like these two words their cry is. They are, like the night-jar, stupid birds to look at, hence in Australia "more-pork" is used as a term of contempt for a stupid person.

It was growing a little light low down in the east before I got to sleep for an hour. When I rose without having rested, I found a small water-hole, took a drink, gave my horse some, and hunted up the road that I had lost in the darkness. By about eight o'clock I came to Grong Grong, and was received by Mr. and Mrs. Morgan and their five daughters with much kindness. Morgan laughed at my adventure with his neighbour. He evidently knew him.

The house was situated in the middle of a grassy plain with here and there clumps of the grey-leaved boree upon it. In the distance this plain was ringed by dark bull and she oaks, and box trees. As yet Morgan had little or no stock on it, save a flock of about a hundred goats, which his daughters milked. They were let out in the morning and generally disappeared from view in the distance. But at sundown the girls went into the open and raised a great shout, an appeal to them to return. In a few moments we could see them tearing across the level plain as hard as they could put hoof to ground. They rushed into their yard at once, and remained quietly when the young ones were parted from their mothers. They had learnt this habit of returning home on being called when the only herd was a ewe goat and two kids.

I remained at Grong Grong a week, giving my horse a good rest, for now I was going further north, and had no friends or acquaintances to call on. As work was so scarce I might travel a long time before getting any chance of a job. It was well to have a fat horse.

When I left Morgan rode with me as far as Mirrool Creek. We saw the superintendent of the station, but he said there was nothing to do just then, and had no need of men. So I shook hands with Morgan and went onward alone. But at night I came to Arriah, and there made the acquaintance of a man who travelled with me to the north of the Lachlan. He was a little Englishman, an educated man who had been an apprentice on board a sailing vessel. As he was going my way, and as I was going very slowly, he came with me. His name was Irving.

The next night we came at dusk to four or five men camped by a water-hole. They were all on foot, and like ourselves were without food. We had all reckoned on making a station, but failing to do so, it seemed that we were to fast that night. Presently, however, one of the men who had a little terrier dog with him, said that he would go and catch a "possum." I did not think what he meant, but the others were more alive to the situation. In about twenty minutes something was cooking in a frying pan carried by one of my temporary mates. We shared it all round. To me it tasted very like mutton, and I said so. There was a general laugh. "How much of the possum did you take, Bill?" said one man.

"Only a quarter."

"And the rest?"

"Threw it in a water-hole," said the hunter.

Of course it was a sheep. He told us that he never went hungry if any "jumbucks" were about, for his dog had learnt the very handy trick of catching a sheep by the hind leg and holding it till his master came up. I believe we were all liable to a term of hard labour for this, for though it is excusable to kill a sheep if one is really starving, none of us could plead that excuse. Before a magistrate my real innocence would not have served me. But it was a very good meal.

The weather now showed very distinct signs of breaking up. Though it had scarcely rained since leaving Wallendool, the sky began to get very threatening. Two days after the incident of the "possum," Irving and I came to Euglo station, on the Euglo or Humbug Creek. We got some grub from the cook, and camped down in the horse paddock, where was fine grass for my horse. By midnight it began to rain heavily, and as from the appearance of the sky that was only the beginning, we bundled up our blankets and made our way in the darkness to the station. We lay down again in a shed which had a roof but no sides. Presently the wind rose and drove the rain in on us; then a stream of water began to course through this poor shelter. We rose again and went into the blacksmith's shop. It was pretty dirty, but almost weather-proof. And the rain came down in bucketfuls.

In the morning the Humbug Creek, which ran right by the station, was almost full to its banks; the smaller horse-paddock was flooded. For three days it never ceased to pour, and I never made the smallest motion to leave quarters which, if not comfortable, were certainly better than the bush in heavy rain. We went into the kitchen and took our meals as if we belonged there. At times we played poker for matches, a mild form of gambling which is quite popular in some parts of the bush. No one did any work. It was an idle time, and I was really glad when the rain held up on the evening of the fourth day. The only work I did for my board and lodging was done then. I held a candle while two men skinned a bullock. In the morning I had to borrow a horse to run mine in, for though he was hobbled, he knew how to gallop in such fetters, and four days' rest with half-wild horses made him very wild himself. I rode away, leaving Irving to follow in a waggon, for there was a very long swamp to cross. After such rain it was not to be accomplished on foot. Even on horseback I had rather a bad time of it. Sometimes Devilskin sank up to his knees and had to free himself with a violent

L

plunge. Once I dropped his bell from my saddle, and getting off to pick it up, I went down more than a foot. But at the end of the three mile swamp we cleaned ourselves by crossing a creek that came up to the saddle flaps. Here I noticed what I have since often found to be true, that a horse generally can tell at once whether a stream is deep enough to render swimming necessary or not, even when the state of the water prevents his rider making more than a rough guess.

On the far side of this creek I came to a sound grassy flat. A half mile canter brought me to a deserted house which was in very good condition though the windows had been taken out. There was a small fenced-in paddock of about two acres, with abundant sweet grass in it. It was an ideal spot to camp. I turned Devilskin loose, and as the sun was now shining I spread out all my clothes and blankets to dry. In an hour Irving came along and joined me. All we now wanted was food, for after staying four days at the Euglo, doing nothing but eat, I lacked the necessary impudence to demand provisions on going away.

But where this house was another must be. The situation of the homestead had been changed, that was all. So saddling up I rode off to find it, taking my bags with me. For bags are as necessary on some roads as a billy: it is not always that squatters will tell one to go to the hut, though they will give generously of their meat and flour. I found it so in this instance. The only one with authority at the station was a woman. On my asking for the boss, she said he was away. Work she had none; tucker, or grub, yes. I went with her. She gave me about seven pounds of flour, two pounds of sugar, nearly half a pound of tea, and when she came to the beef I had to check her. I could not carry more than a lump weighing ten pounds. I saw that very few travellers came that way, and told her so. She smiled and said she had not seen any but me for weeks. I thanked her for the food and went back to Irving. We had enough for a week, and did not shift our quarters for three days.

This was very easy travelling. Yet what was the use of being in a hurry? No one seemed to want hands. It really began to get sickening asking for work. We might just as well lie down and smoke and look at the sun and drink in the air. But at last we tired of doing nothing and went on.

The next day we saw a curious and charming sight as we went through a great paddock thinly touched here and there with trees. As Irving and I talked we heard a noise behind us, and stayed, turning to listen. The low roar we heard was not that of loosed waters, nor that of a great wind, nor of distant thunder. Yet it was like all these. I turned my horse towards an advancing cloud of dust which came towards us furiously. He quivered in every limb. It was instinct, but not the instinct of fear.

The line, which came closer and closer yet, was about twenty yards wide upon the dusty plain which we had just left to enter upon a long stretch of comparatively sound and grassy country; and as the sand gradually gave way to the thicker herbage, so the swirling cloud that hung over the unseen squadron was dissipated until through its thinner veil we caught sight at length of outstretched horses' heads. For it was of these that the squadron was formed. How many there were it was at first impossible even to guess, but as they emerged from the dust in a wide loose column, we saw there were at least hundreds coming on with a thunder of hoof which was almost terrifying in its swift approaching increase. They were all colours, from black to bright chestnut, to bay and grey and white: their manes and tails were flying, and their eyes flashed in the light of the northern sun at noon behind us. No one was driving them, they were drawn by desire, not driven by fear, and as they came nearer and nearer my horse snatched at his bit. He was wild with excitement and would join those his free companions. He reared violently as I checked him, and stood pawing the air while the riderless cavalry came within fifty yards of us and performed a sudden, beautiful evolution which made us shout for joy. The front line of the column stopped as though at some signal, and from both sides those behind shot out into a curve until we were in the centre of a long semicircle of horses some two deep, who burst with one accord into a great chorus of whinnies and neighs which seemed to ask who and what we were, and to invite Devilskin to get rid of his rider and join the ranks of the free.

Throwing up his head he answered them loudly, and for a moment I feared the invitation would be accepted. But at last he quietened down, and I had time to look at the wild mob in front of us, which gradually broke from its orderly formation as two or three stallions and the most curious of the others approached us more nearly. These came up to within a few yards, and, turning round suddenly, galloped away at the smallest motion we made, while the rest squealed and kicked and bit and played until the noise they made was deafening. Then at last their curiosity was sated and they began to draw off in loose order. I turned my horse's head northward and we resumed our journey. We had not gone a mile before we heard the thunder of their hoofs again as they came after us in a long column some ten wide at the head. On reaching us they again halted suddenly, and shot out into the wide-winged curve. But now I had seen enough of them, and, disengaging my stockwhip, I cracked it loudly. At the very first report they threw up their heads, wheeled round, and were in rapid flight across the plain. They followed us no more. In the afternoon of that day I was offered the first job since leaving Yarra Yarra. But as it was bullock-driving at fifteen shillings a week, less by ten shillings than the normal wages for such work, I refused it at once.

That night we came to the Lachlan. Across it we saw the little bush township of Condobolin.

The Australian rivers vary somewhat in character, but after they leave the hill country in which they rise, they generally assume the aspect of slow, deep streams within high banks on which grow such gum-trees as rise to a great altitude by rivers or a chain of water-holes. No one seeing the Lachlan in its later summer quietude could imagine that it ever became vigorous and energetic, and the evening Irving and I made our camp upon its banks it was dumb and motionless. We stayed near a little "tin house" made of corrugated iron, which was occupied by a solitary man and surrounded by fairly good grass, and when I climbed down the steep river-bank to obtain water for tea-making I could hardly discern which way the river flowed. But as we smoked with the hut-dweller after supper, a horseman came along. He pulled up at the door.

"I hear," said he, "that the river is rising fast

above Forbes. They say there is a good deal of water coming down."

I took but little notice of the ensuing conversation and soon after curled up in my blankets under a big gum, while my horse picked up a plentiful repast near the banks of the river. When I woke in the morning very early, just as the dawn showed very faintly through the heavy sombre foliage, I became aware of a slight and unusual sound. It was rather a hiss than a roar, even though distant. I fancied it might be the light air stirring the top branches of the gums, but when I turned over towards the Lachlan, whose banks were but fifteen yards away, I saw a pool of water, which I knew had not been there the evening before, between me and the sloping edge of the stream. I recalled the words of last night's traveller, and knew that the mountain flood must have reached us on the plains. I rose and went towards it. The sight was a curious one.

In a long, grey, level country, like the greater portion of western New South Wales, a turbulent or eager river is a novelty. Last night the stream had moved on lazily and with reluctance, a leaf dropped on its still surface by an opossum in the boughs of an overhanging tree stayed in the same spot for many minutes, or if it did move it was with such a slight progression that it mocked one's powers of measurement and deceived the eye into believing the still waters in those deep banks were no more than a pool or long lagoon. But now the great gap between bank and bank was filled with a strong and energetic flood which rushed onward steadily and only stayed in those places where it flowed out upon the level. The river yesterday was pellucid, now it was as turbid as a street torrent. By an optical delusion the stream's centre seemed higher than the sides; in the middle was a wide streak of dirty foam, which half hid the leaves, sticks and branches the flood had collected from the sloping banks for hundreds of miles, as well as a few drowned sheep and here and there a bullock or horse, suddenly surprised in a place whence escape was impossible. The day before the river had been dead, now it was strong, alive, palpitating : it possessed being, and power, and faculties ; it could do things, and speak ; it had a soul and a voice ; the mountains far away to the eastward, where Australia leaps at last from the level, had given it a mission and imparted to it some of the primæval strength that dwells in the regions of snow and tropical rain. It looked to me like an irruption of northerners into the realms of luxurious Rome, an invasion of a summer Sybaris, a warning and an awakening in a slothful land of the lotus, for as I stood and watched it, half in a dream, it seemed to send my own blood faster by a strong suggestion and sympathy. It was with difficulty that I tore myself away to make ready for the day's journey.

In the middle of the following day we came to Forbes, the scene of the once famous Lachlan gold diggings. It was a town of dead gold-fields and dead tree-stumps. Though it seemed active enough from a business point of view in the heart of the town, in the outskirts an abomination of desolation reigned. The piles of white earth ejected and rejected from the silent pits of deserted mines, no longer thronged by eager men; the thousands of dead, stricken, and destroyed trees only evidenced by ghastly stumps, made me anxious to get away from the largest town I had seen since leaving Albury on the Murray. For here humanity was mainly manifest by the outrages it had committed on nature, the town itself seemed but a small, ugly parasite fattening on the carcase of the once flourishing forest, and seeing the evil works of civilized man, I preferred going farther into the wilderness. So, after vainly asking for letters at the post-office, we turned westward again, going down the Lachlan, which was now rapidly falling in volume and failing in energy. We camped in a silent, untouched forest of gum-trees.

CHAPTER IX.

BURRAWANG.

By this time, if I reckoned from the date on which I left Albury, I had been on the road, looking for work, for three months. I had asked a hundred times for something or for anything to do, along three hundred and fifty miles of country, and had asked in vain. I was now without money, though that does not matter much in most parts of New South Wales, and was almost in despair as to getting work. Irving and I had, indeed, come to the resolution to ask no more if we failed at the next place. We elaborated a gigantic scheme which included selling my horse and getting some kind of a boat in which to navigate the Lachlan or Darling right through New South Wales to Adelaide. But fate was kind, and did not send us to encounter the difficulties which would have awaited us at every turn of such a journey, for we came to Burrawang.

At this big "station" every one was in violent activity. Building was going on at a great rate and new foundations were being dug for an immense hut to shelter all the employés, while horses and carts and horsemen were as busy as though it were the headquarters of an army preparing for winter. The prospect seemed encouraging for men willing to work, and in ten minutes we were both engaged, for I tackled one "boss" after the other until finally I came to the owner of the place. He stared at me for half a moment and then said—

"Yes; you go out to the Deadman Plain, both of you. Be at the store at one o'clock and go with Ross."

We had not the least notion what we were to do, and it was only when we were in the waggon on our way to the plain so disagreeably named that we found that our destined task was "burr cutting." It required some further explanation to satisfy me, for I knew not what burrs were nor why they should be cut. There is, as it appeared, a kind of harmful plant which grows increasing on the plains of New South Wales. It is known as the Bathurst Burr, and is a great nuisance to wool-growers, as the burrs get knotted in the sheep's coats, and by making the wool hard to comb render it much less valuable. By Act of the Legislature, squatters are required to cut it down ere it sheds its seeds and burn it. We had come just in time for the burr-cutting season, and were soon hard at it with a hoe apiece.

Our camp was close to Deadman Plain, which was so named from a traveller dying there of thirst, and only divided from it by a thin belt of bull and she oaks and dry sombre-looking dwarf box-trees. Our tents were comfortable, we had a good cook and good rations, and we drew good water from a shallow lagoon enlarged artificially by a dam. To this lake came black swans and spoonbills, with smaller water-fowl. At night time what we called curlews flew overhead and made the melancholy plain ring with their fearful screams, which suggest hideous massacres of unarmed people. I know no more dreadful note in all nature. But curlews they certainly were not. Our ornithology was at fault. Curiously enough I have no desire to identify them in a long list of names. It is enough that I heard them cry at midnight in a strange land, which is sombre and melancholy even at noon. Being unknown, they make it more mysterious yet, and almost spiritual. Every tree about us was plentifully provided with opossums, who stole at night into our tents; and every day we saw kangaroo, and their lesser relatives the nocturnal kangaroo-rats, which we disturbed in their sleep as we worked on the plain. They usually camp in little hollows of the ground, and carefully cover themselves with dry grass, in order to protect themselves from the fierce sun, or to hide from the eagles which for ever fly round overhead looking for such game or a lamb or sick sheep. For these birds poison baits were specially laid, and we often came across a splendid dead specimen destroyed in this way. Not infrequently pigs which had run wild and multiplied in the bush were also poisoned. There was certainly plenty of animal life about our camp. We did not keep dogs, as it was necessary to have them closely muzzled on account of the baits which were lying everywhere about us.

The great "eagle hawks" of this country are of the species *Aquila fucosa*, according to Gould. They were very numerous. At any hour of the day I could count a dozen circling high above the plain. Occasionally they swooped down to the ground, and then I knew that they had descried a stray lamb, or a ewe in labour, or a piece of carrion, for noble as these birds are in appearance they do not disdain dead food. Thus they are easy to poison.

One evening, when I and another man were making our way home through a belt of bull-oaks, we saw a very large eagle on the ground. He made an abortive attempt to rise, but fell back and let us approach without making any demonstration. But he watched us very keenly. He had evidently been poisoned, yet showed no signs of pain, his eye was fierce and bright, and the clutch of his sharp talons as strong as ever. When I put a stick near him he grasped it tightly, so tightly indeed that I could scarcely make him let go. To me, it seemed a great pity that so fine and noble a bird should meet such a miserable and unnatural end. I proposed to my mate that we should carry him to the camp, which was about a quarter of a mile away, give him some water, and see if he would not recover. For, as I have said, there were no signs of death about him. The result of the poison was no more than a kind of paralysis. It was no easy task to take the eagle captive. Indeed, if it had not been for

his fierce grasp of the stick, which he refused to let go, I doubt whether we should have been able to carry him. After some difficulty, being in no little danger of receiving a terrible snap from his beak, I got him by the neck, put a strap round his legs, and thus we carried him between us on a pole. When we reached the camp I offered him water which he refused. I loosed his legs, managed to keep the strap on one, and tied him with a short tether. In the morning he was dead. This particular bird was a very fine specimen, and would have been well worth skinning if I had been a practised hand at such work. His weight was I should think nearly fifteen pounds, the spread of the wings almost seven feet.

I suppose from the point of view of the sheep-owner these eagles are but noxious and destructive vermin. Yet it seems a vile thing to poison such beautiful birds, often the only living things to be seen on the plains or over them, when the hot days make the low-flying birds glad to seek the heavy shadows of the oak belts, while no animal shows in the sun. But of course we want wool and mutton. No one needs eagles. They are a luxury even for an ornithologist, and one he hardly expects to get. Soon, when Australia is one vast meat farm, this dun-coloured eagle, with his lofty flight, and swift stoop, with his terrible beak and talons, will become rare. Towards the south of New South Wales and in Victoria it is no longer common; there the sheep-owners have no need to use strychnine.

One day, or rather afternoon, as we were working on the far side of Deadman's Plain, a kangaroo-rat sprang out of a hollow, thrusting aside the bunch of grass with which it was concealed. The man who had disturbed it was a swift runner. He dropped his hoe and chased it. Soon it became evident that he was actually coming up with the flying marsupial, until the wretched animal, which was a female, put its fore-paw into its pouch and threw away its young one, or in Australian parlance " dinged the joey." This little joey I caught at once. It was a soft, beautiful little thing, and being loth to leave it or even to mercifully kill it, I opened my shirt and put it next my skin. It nestled down at once as if in its mother's pouch. I carried it thus till knock-off time. The men chaffed me a little, asking how I liked being a mother kangaroo-rat, but they were all pleased to see my joey when it peeped out and then suddenly retreated. All kangaroos and wallabies are very easily tamed, and this youngster was no exception. When we reached the camp I put him on the ground and he hopped about as if quite at home. The cook, a rough old English sailor, was so delighted with the little animal that he begged it of me, and as it is at all times and in all places good to be a *persona grata* with the *chef*, I parted with my pet, though not without some reluctance. But the cook being at the camp all day had a better chance to look after him. He made a bed of dry grass for him in a box in his tent. At night-time as we had supper, the joey would hop out and pick up crumbs. If he heard any alarming noise in two jumps he was in his box covered up with the grass.

During six weeks of the late summer Irving and I worked hard at burr cutting for the regulation wages of a pound a week. We hoed them down, raked them together in heaps to dry, and finally made great bonfires of them under the burning Australian sun, which is always hot whenever it shines, even though it be only a cloudless interval of the rainy

season. The heat was frequently intense, but I found, as is so often the case, that I endured it better than the native-born whites themselves, of whom we had several representative specimens in the camp.

Men born and reared in wild countries are rarely well educated in any sense of the word, but after a varied experience of all sorts and conditions of Texans, Californians, British Columbians, and many others, commend me to a bush-bred New South Wales man for sheer downright ignorance. I by no means attempted to set up as an authority or a dictator of debates, and yet I was continually getting into trouble by innocently introducing what my mates considered new and dangerous heresies.

For instance, I one day let fall a remark which implied that the world was round. If I remember rightly I said that England was nearly beneath us. This caused a most violent commotion in the circle seated round the camp-fire near our lagoon. The elder of two brothers—both very big men and hostile to me on account of other strange theories—was so righteously indignant with me that for a moment I feared I had said something which hurt his feelings. When he had discovered by questions that I was not joking, he looked at me solemnly and with great self-control quoted the Bible. I made some innocent remarks about Biblical and other early cosmogonies which the whole company considered impious and heretical. I began to feel like Galileo before the Inquisition. I wondered whether I was in a tribe of savages or whether my education had been conducted on a radically wrong basis. They plied me with questions, threw ridicule on me, used the rudest species of bush irony and backwoods sarcasm, and when I appealed in despair to Irving to support my view of the universe, they begged me to leave him alone, as they felt certain he was not such a fool as to believe anything so absurdly, so ridiculously, so impiously and startlingly new as my theory. I grew angry and retorted, used all the well-known arguments, asked them questions in return, and at last hit on one which nobody could answer. Then Big Bill rose up in wrath, and, backed by his brother and the applause of the crowd, actually threatened to go for me then and there if I did not refrain from the promulgation of blatant atheism. As I saw no prospect of being able to fight the whole camp with any satisfactory result, I retired, like Achilles, to my tent, and smoked in silent and solitary indignation.

If I had been a little older I might have known better than expect intelligence from a gang whose sole talk was of horses, varied not infrequently with the vilest ribaldry. Should my evil destiny ever drive me again among Australians of that sort, I am prepared to acknowledge that the cutting of burrs is a necessary preliminary to the study of philosophy, and will without demur subscribe to the Cartesian theory of vortices or to the ancient cosmogony of Ptolemy. When I have grown so meek I shall never attempt to defend school astronomy, nor will I fight for any new-fangled geographical theory whatever.

Why it is I cannot say, but there is little or no reading done in the Australian bush. In America one may always find the best novels—of course in pirated editions—in every store. I have bought Thomas Hardy's *Far from the Madding Crowd*, and George Meredith's *Diana of the Crossways* on a counter covered with bear hides in a little British Columbian store by the Shushwap Lake, but I never found any literature in the New South Wales bush. A weekly newspaper is as far as one may go there.

As it was, I did not get away from Deadman's Plain without a desperate fight, in which I got satisfactorily whipped after putting my thumb out of joint. The cause of the combat was neither evolution nor history, but language. And language of a kind which according to bush ethics left me with no peaceful alternative. I had been suffering from an ulcerated throat, and had eaten nothing solid for a week. When I recovered I restored the balance of power, and a week afterwards triumphantly fired the last dried heap of cut burrs and went back to the Home Station.

I had entertained some hope of employment for the whole of the winter, or rainy season, which was just setting in; but was disappointed. Apparently the great business of the year was over, and I received my cheque, or what is called in bush parlance my " walking papers." Fortunately, I had my horse, and so had a man with whom I made chums, who had just been sacked for fighting with his boss. Charlie McPhillamy was a young Victorian, a rather melancholy ne'er-do-well, who began at twenty-nine to regret having lost what opportunities Fate had afforded him, in the desolation of the grey-brown plains of New South Wales. Yet he was an amiable, well-dispositioned fellow, whom I liked much, and should have liked far better if it had not been for his ineradicable desire to get up early. All my life I have abhorred that most unnatural proceeding; in all my wanderings and strange tasks the necessity for getting up with the fanatical sun has been the most bitter of all bitternesses to me, and now I make up for it by remaining in bed, if I possibly can, while I reflect with satisfaction that no ranch bell rings, no saw-mill whistle blows, no watch on deck roar " Starbowlines ahoy ! " no bo'son sings out " Turn to ! " and that no boss of any description whatever comes to threaten me with the sack if I don't mend my morning manners. I sometimes hated McPhillamy for rousing me, and once I chased him with a stirrup I snatched from my saddle. For early rising in Australia when travelling in the rainy season was wholly unnecessary. Still he was a very good fellow, and a man more after my heart than Irving, who remained behind at Burrawang when I left.

CHAPTER X.

TOWARDS THE WILLANDRA.

THE weather was now really going to break up in earnest. As Charlie and I rode out of Burrawang the sky was heavily clouded. Yet the rain did not come just yet. My new mate and I held a consultation as to where we should go. This was almost a matter of indifference to me so long as it was not where I had been before. But Charlie had got over his earlier desire for adventure and new things. Accordingly he suggested going west. How far, I asked. A couple of hundred miles or so. He had worked on a station called Mossgiel, well out in the Lachlan Back Blocks, as the country far from the river is called. I was quite willing, and accordingly we turned our horses' heads towards the west and followed the Lachlan down for some miles. One night we camped opposite Condobolin, in a wretched ramshackle old hut, with a companion whom I seemed to know. After some conversation it turned out that I had met him the year before on the Murray River, more than three hundred miles to the southward, when he was in a state of prosperity—fat, well-dressed, with a good horse, having charge of a mob of travelling sheep. Now he was on foot, in rags, carrying his blankets and cooking a little flour, affording a good example of the sudden changes of condition so often witnessed in new countries and usually to be traced to drink or gambling.

That night our horses took a little stroll all on their own account, and in the morning were not to be seen. I took up their trail, as I thought, and followed it for about seven miles through thick bush, often getting thrown off the scent, but as often finding it again. I was sure that they were our horses, because Charlie's animal dragged his near forefoot the veriest trifle, making a peculiar mark, but when I at last came up with them I found, to my intense disgust, that they were not ours. I had been tracking from eight o'clock in the morning until two, and had to wearily retrace my steps. Charlie I found recumbent in the hut, smoking with melancholy satisfaction that it was not he who was in the bush, but he did not look so pleased when he saw me limp in, tired, disgusted and unsuccessful. After a rest I took the billy and went down to the river, which was about eighty yards away, and close to the banks I found the horses I had walked fourteen miles for. If I fancied my own wicked animal, Devilskin, leered with satisfaction and was fat with self-conceit, I may not have been far out, for he certainly knew a thing or two about travelling.

In the next township I bought a bell for his neck. My last one I lost at the Horse Lagoon before coming to Burrawang. But he played me a different trick soon afterwards, which the bell did not serve to prevent.

That day was the last fine weather we had. In the evening it came on to rain heavily, and henceforward, for six weeks, there were few hours that the sky was not lowering. It is not pleasant work, riding along for a whole day, wet through, but when a day multiplies itself indefinitely, and a dry skin becomes a kind of legend or myth in one's personal history, the infliction has a tendency to depress the strongest traveller. We rarely came to a travellers' hut, the stations were thinly scattered, and to stay in the hotels at an occasional township which consisted of a general store, a drinking house and a blacksmith's shop, was decidedly hard on one's purse. Ours were not very heavy, for though Charlie left Burrawang with ten pounds, I had only five. So we usually camped out in the open or under the gums, which are not a whit more satisfactory as shelter-trees than the straggling cedars of the Pacific slope in British Columbia. They do no more than concentrate the rain and pour it on you in spouts rather than in sprinkles. Yet there is a certain satisfaction in being under a big tree; one can make believe that he has something over him, and, trusting to his imagination, may pity the poor fellows who that night are forced to camp on the open plain.

For a week it rained, and then for another week, until the ground, which at no time was hard or rocky, became saturated, and so soft that the horses went in over the hoofs, and we wretched individuals woke up in the morning to find that we lay in pools of warm muddy water. During the whole journey Charlie was eager to rise betimes. It may seem that he was wise, seeing the state of affairs;

but if so I was foolish. The weather was not very cold, my blankets were new and heavy (they are the same I took all over Western America and I possess them now), and I was fond of sleep. I did not mind being wet so long as I was warm, and I used to refuse to rise on any pretext. Charlie would get up, go away and then come back and relate to me through the blankets which covered my head, that he believed our horses were lost. I replied sleepily that I was glad of it, and wished he would go and lose himself too. Yet it was in vain. I had to rise, sulkily, at last. Then, to add insult to injury, I could by no persuasion get him ready to leave camp. As long as I was up he didn't care, and would do nothing. It fell to me to seek the horses: often and often I saddled his as well as my own, and sometimes I rode off a mile, leaving him lazily contemplating his wet gear or hunting for a hot coal to light the fourth pipe he had smoked since rising. Certainly we did not work well together.

One night we came to a nice little bend in the river where there was plenty of grass and an immense quantity of fallen dead timber. The gum trees there were particularly large for that part of the country, some of them measuring fifteen feet or more in girth. We selected this place for a camp and turned our horses loose. We started a fire under a great trunk, determined, since it still rained, and was comparatively cold, that we would for once have a real blaze. Charlie and I carried wood for an hour, and by nine o'clock the flames shot twenty feet into the air, roaring and hissing with the falling rain, while the leaves of the gum trees above turned brown with the parching heat. For once in a while we were dry. But in the morning my horse was gone, bell and all. Charlie's nag stared at us disconsolately when we found him, but he was decidedly alone. For three days my mate hunted the absentee, and when he was just on the point of giving up the search, he discovered him in a large mob of horses belonging to the station on which we were camped. He drove them all into the stockyard and I parted Devilskin from the rest with some trouble. When I saddled him he was nearly wild and bucked violently, so excited was he by his temporary intercourse with the half-wild strangers. Then in the morning my mate's horse was missing. This was a heavy blow to us, for we wanted to get on. It took three days to find him. When we finally did leave that unlucky bend we went into a wretched little township a few miles farther down the river and stayed at the hotel, where they charged us seven-and-sixpence apiece for the entertainment of our horses on what is known as "hay" in that part of the bush, that is, barley in the straw.

In the morning we started off, and came by night, in the rain, to the most wretched camping-ground we had yet had. It resembled a swamp; indeed, it was partly covered with a kind of reed or cane-brake, which only grows in damp situations. The added rain made the place terrible indeed. We tried to go on, but with the falling darkness much more travel was out of the question. Besides, the farther we went the worse it got. At last we camped in despair, and chose the only sloping piece of ground we could see, which was by a big rain-pool. Suitable wood there was none, and all there was seemed proof against fire, for weeks of soaking had saturated it. Charlie, who had been much longer in the bush than I, was more hopeless of a blaze. He affirmed that we could not get one without an axe, or a tomahawk at the least, and we possessed neither. But I would not camp out without a fire. I took my knife, and going to the trees, peeled off the outside bark, which I rejected, but taking the under layer, scraped it up and put it inside my shirt. I chose the most sheltered spot of ground I could find and turned over the leaves until I came to a layer of those which were less wet than the others. I put them with the bark. Going round to the gathering darkness, I rattled the bush about to find dead twigs, which I broke into small pieces and pouched as well. Then I returned to my mate, who was sitting on his saddle in a state of gloom, with the heavy rain pouring over him. I asked him for paper — a letter, an envelope, anything. He had none. I had none

myself, so at last I was compelled to cut away part of the only match-box I had and shred it up fine. By this time I was very damp, and my fire materials, though they made me very uncomfortable, seemed dryer. I scraped a little spot clear, and making Charlie hold his hat over it, put my paper down.

This I covered with a few leaves. Match after match went out, but each one that did so dried the materials a little, besides going on the pile, and at last I got a little blaze. By careful attention I preserved it so that it grew, adding leaf by leaf and twig by twig, until Charlie was able to put his hat on again. In an hour we had a fine fire, and were able to turn our attention to making the tea, without which every travelling Australian is a miserable rebellious animal against destiny.

Meantime the rain came down in torrents. We were, of course, saturated, our blankets were heavy, the ground squelched with every step we made and squirted liquid mud. I took Charlie's blankets with one of my own and spread them on the sloping ground, while I fixed some rude poles and a horizontal stick, upon which I placed my other blanket. With my hands I scraped a rough trench at the top, and carried it round at the sides. The fire was at our feet, and we crawled in very carefully to avoid bringing down the canopy. The bed was at any rate soft, so much could be said for it, for I felt myself sinking as if I were on feathers. The fire being fairly hot, and the two of us close together, we managed to keep warm, finally going to sleep steaming in a kind of mingled mud and rain bath. For very soon the water came through the upper blanket.

In the middle of the night I woke up feeling very cold and uncomfortable. Stretching out my hand I found that the trench above had so altered its configuration that it concentrated the water and delivered it on me in one volume. A little more and I should have slid out of the impromptu tent. I growled and plastered vainly at the trench with mud which was too liquid to dam the breach, and in my struggles I dislodged the sticks, letting the canopy and horizontal down on Charlie. He woke up and looked into matters. Finally we rejected the sticks, let the upper blanket remain where it was, rolled close together, and determined to take what fate sent. So I slept again in a running stream.

In the early morning we crawled out, looking two more wretched mortals than any Prometheus brought fire to. We were plastered with mud and running with water. Neither could have been moister if he had slept in the rising pool which hissed now in the lower embers of our sinking fire. I took hold of the blankets and ripped them from the ground, which then showed deep casts of our figures. As they could not be wetter, and might be cleaner, we washed them in the pool, wrung them out, and wore them as ponchos or cloaks. In sombre silence we looked to the fire, made tea, saddled up and departed, The next day we came to the Willandra Billabong.

So far as I am aware there is no similar feature to the true billabong in any country except Australia. Certainly there are rivers whose raised banks only restrain them from flooding the adjacent districts, such as the Po, and other streams of northern Italy ;

but to this end human labour has been employed during many centuries in heightening the natural barriers which grow less and less efficacious as the detritus and wash from the Alps fill their beds in the lower valleys and plains. In Australia the level of some of the rivers at flood time is decidedly above the level of the neighbouring districts, and the billabongs found in the Lachlan and other streams are natural aqueducts, like the lashers of some of our rivers, artificially raised by locks, which draw off the water when it rises to a certain level. On reaching the Willandra Charley McPhillamy, who was familiar with that part of New South Wales, pointed out to me what had all the appearance of a dry affluent to the river by which we had been journeying, and asked me what I thought of it. I said it was a "creek," or stream-bed, then dry. It certainly seemed to be what I said, and yet, in spite of its look, no water ever ran from it into the river. On the contrary, as I soon found out, when the river rose as it had done when I was travelling with Irving, the turbid waters poured out into the country by this gap and ran like an original stream through three hundred miles of plain which had otherwise been wholly dependent on rain and dug wells for its supply.

That night we stayed at the junction of the Willandra with the Lachlan, camping at a very good travellers' hut. The boss of the station gave us meat and flour, and as three other men were likewise camped there, we made up quite a small party to discuss work and the weather, and the probability of water from the river getting into the Billabong that year. In the morning, on going to the Lachlan for water I passed a wretched old black fellow camped in a bit of a gunyah or native hut with his two wives. He was very urgent that I should give him some tobacco, and offered various inducements which did not in the least tempt me. In the morning we turned down the Willandra, for Mossgiel is on the Billabong, and that night, after no very long ride, we stayed on a barren-looking, open salt bush plain, at a grog shanty known as Bale's Hotel. We were now well into the salt bush country. On this salty, but succulent thick-leaved plant sheep flourish admirably. In the hotel we did not flourish, for both of us had something there described as brandy, but known to colonials as "sheepwash." It is said that in order to make the vile concoction take quicker effect on the unwary tobacco is put in the cask. Certainly, three small drinks made me feel as if I had been poisoned, and Charlie, who took more, was ill for four or five days afterwards.

The country we were now in could hardly be described as interesting. On leaving the Lachlan we quitted the region of the big gums, while the box trees grew smaller and more dwarfed yet as we got into the heart of of the plains in the Back Blocks. The billabong was then almost empty, save for a few pools here and there; its banks and beds were covered with dry wind-shaken reeds, around us everywhere was a boundless level, only broken by a few stray clumps of dismal dwarf boxes that could be seen, though not larger in girth than nine inches, very many miles away. Fortunately for us, the weather changed a little; it no longer rained in ceaseless torrents; the sky, though sometimes overcast and rarely free from clouds, was not a dismal canopy of leaden hue; the sun often shone cheerfully and we were rarely quite wet to the skin. But we had a week's journey before us yet, and having started from the separation of the river and billabong with nothing but flour and some jam in our commissariat, we found at the only place we expected to get meat that the occupants of the hut were just then no better provided with flesh foods than ourselves.

There is such a thing as being hungry and not being able to eat certain foods. I found that existing five days on bread and jam while riding in the open plains, or while occupying oneself for a day or so in succession hunting up a strayed horse was almost as unpleasant as the absolute and horrible starvation I was yet to experience. I loathed the bread made in thin cakes on the coals, known in the colonies as Johnny-cakes, and as for jam, I think I have not yet recovered my liking for it. We were both almost ready to steal a sheep, so keen grew our carnivorous desires. In the end we absolutely refused to touch what we had left and rode on fiercely, knowing that we could not be very far from the

Mossgiel sheep-shed, by which some Chinamen were living. We reached their huts at last, late in the evening.

I dismounted and walked up to the place. Peering into the dirty interior, dimly lighted by the bush light called a slush-lamp, I spied four Chinamen playing euchre with a pack of almost indistinguishable cards. They looked up rather sulkily on being disturbed. I asked for meat, or rather demanded it, having previously made up my mind that if there was any to be had, I would obtain it at any cost, even by fighting. They denied  they had any, but as I saw a dried piece of sheep ribs hanging on a hook, I seized hold of it without any circumlocution and asked how much they wanted. On payment of a shilling I departed with my prize, and we repaired to the shearers' hut, at that time of the year quite empty.

We were perfectly ravenous. It was dry salt meat, but to think of wasting time in boiling it was ludicrous. We found a rude gridiron made of fencing wire in the old hut's fireplace and began grilling. I ate fifteen small chops in rapid succession, and Charlie finished the remainder. Though the saltness of it was indescribable, I never enjoyed a meal more in all my life, and shall probably never do so again until I ride a hundred miles in keen bright air living on bread and jam. But during the whole night I was drinking water. In the morning the door of our sleeping hut was burst violently open and a big black-and-tan collie rushed in. He made instant overtures of affection to me and ended by leaping into my bunk, where he lay until the boundary rider who lived close by called to him.

For breakfast we ate the remainder of the salt mutton and some flat bread cakes given us by this same boundary rider. The seven miles between the shearing shed and Mossgiel we accomplished in a leisurely fashion and reached the home station by about eight. The boss on being appealed to in the customary manner, gave Charlie his old job of boundary riding, and asked me if I could kill sheep and milk. Without any hesitation I said I could and was hired. I had never milked a cow in my life. The only time I had ever tried was at Mahonga and, though Annie tried her best to teach me, the art remained occult and unattainable. But I was tired of travelling and would at least try.

CHAPTER XI.

THE LAND OF SHEEP.

Much to my surprise I found that I could milk without any difficulty. It is true that my hands grew very tired at first but that soon wore off. I became dexterous in a week, and could without trouble always supply the two buckets of milk needed for the house and have a little over for the men's hut. This was a very small quantity to get from six cows, but then in the bush, especially far up from town, cows are not bred especially for milking purposes. The butchering was an odious job, one which I was with difficulty reconciled to. Even now I hate to think of it. The demands for meat in a meat-eating country with some fifty men to keep supplied often gave me a hard tussle. But at last I became dexterous even at that, learnt to use the knife in both hands, and could give several minutes to any one on the station. I disliked both jobs but the milking was least disagreeable.

Yet even in that I had much trouble. They were continually taking away quiet cows for some out station, and to replace these they sent me wild ones to break in. A young cow with her first calf is an awkward customer to handle and I often sat on the fence wondering how to begin with an animal which showed a strong and pointed disinclination to let me enter the yard at all. But there is a way to do everything and fortunately a cow can be roped from a distance. Occasionally when that failed, and no one in Australia is really clever with the lasso, I had to go in and let the cow charge me. It happens that any beast can be knocked down and stunned if struck in the proper place; and in cows and bullocks this is just behind the horns. So I took a stick about a yard long which was rather supple, and an inch and a half through at the thick end. As the cow charged I jumped aside, struck her, and as she lay put the rope over her horns. It was sometimes rather dangerous work. But at any rate it was exciting and afforded some compensation for the monotony of a job which often left much time on my hands and no means of occupying it.

In this part of the country there were usually a

good many black fellows. They camped at the back of the station, towards the north, and the gins or women always came to me begging for the sheep's heads. As colonials do not care for any but the very best parts of the mutton, I was always at liberty to give them away. These black fellows were for the most part a very miserable lot, though there were a few bright young boys among them and some very tall men. One called Moses, out-topped me by an inch. He took a sort of liking for me, and once or twice made me a stock whip-handle out of a piece of myall wood. But he never forgot to apply for some silver afterwards. The women were mostly of a hideousness on a par with their mental and moral status. Only one, a tall girl known as Catherine, who always dressed in loose calico gown and nothing besides, was passably good-looking, and she was invariably intoxicated. If there is any such law in New South Wales as they have in British Columbia forbidding the gift or sale of liquor to the aborigines, I never knew it enforced. But they are a doomed race, and cannot exist for long, even if our pleasant civilization be restrained from destroying them by its vices. I cannot regret the women, but some of the men were really fine fellows in their way, and wonderfully keen and intelligent.

After working very regularly at my new job for nearly two months I began to sicken of it most heartily. I think if I had still had my horse I should have asked for my cheque and saddled up. But

I sold Devilskin to the man who had been milkman before I came, and got a very good price for him, £13. Horses on these plains are much more valuable than in the hills. However, I went to the boss, who was now Mr. Webster, formerly of Round Hill, north of Albury and near Burrumbuttock, and asked to be given the next vacancy as boundary rider. He promised it to me as soon as any likely traveller came along to replace me. This happened the next week, just at the very time a boundary rider left the Strathavon out-station, fourteen miles to the southward of Mossgiel. I initiated the new man into the mysteries, showed him where he was most likely to find the cows in the big horse paddock, rolled up my blankets, and went south to occupy the loftier and more generally esteemed position of a man whose duty was to ride.

For in the bush there is something of the same feeling which distinguishes cavalrymen from linesmen. A dragoon despises a foot-soldier; "infantry swine" is a common term of abuse in the army. It is almost the same among the workers in the Colonies. I felt it a distinct rise in society to be a boundary rider, but soon discovered that the common impression that a horseman's work was no work at all was quite a delusion. "Just sitting on a horse" was very decidedly work, when the ordinary day's ride was rarely less than thirty miles and often nearer fifty. And on extraordinary occasions, when we mustered sheep in the great paddocks ten miles square, I sometimes covered eighty or ninety miles in the day.

For Mossgiel was a great station which stretched far away to the north and south, and consisted of 1,100 square miles of territory, or 700,000 acres. On this vast salt bush plain roamed hundreds of thousands of sheep. In the three paddocks whose fences I was responsible for were about thirty-five thousand, and by the end of lambing nearly fifty thousand. For sixteen thousand in one paddock were ewes, and our lambing percentage was that year over a hundred. My outside fences were fifty miles round.

At Strathavon the overseer had a small house, as he was a married man with a young family, while I lived in a tent, and did my own cooking; my mate was mostly an oldish man, called Veale, who was comparatively wealthy, though he worked as I did for a pound a week and his grub. He had had some three thousand pounds left him by a relative in England, but showed no signs of leaving off hard work.

My work at first was not very arduous as I was used to riding. I usually went round one paddock a day to see if any of the wires were broken. Occasionally a kangaroo got trapped in them as he came along in the dark. The kangaroos of the plains are reddish in colour, not grey as their congeners of the hills or wooded country. Then there were numbers of emus everywhere. It was curious to see them running along the plain in single file. Few horses can run the older birds down, but I once captured a youngster by coiling my stock-whip round its neck. They grow as tame and impudent as a pet kangaroo or lamb. These emus I frequently found in the fences, for when they put a leg through on one side and toppled over on the other, the twisted wires held them like a vice. On these rides I carried wire tools, a nipper for cutting, and a piece of iron with holes in it to twist together, or splice the broken wires. If posts were knocked down, I told Veale on my return home, and he went out with a bar and shovel to set them up again. This was practically all my work for nearly three months. My long leisure time I spent in reading, and reading again all the books I could get. As they were few, I read them over till I knew them by heart.

My best companion—for after all Veale was but a thick-headed worker—was my dog Sancho, the very colley who was the first inhabitant of Mossgiel to greet me as I and Charlie McPhillamy slept in the shearers' hut. His owner left the station, and sold him to me for three pounds. I had another young dog I had brought from Mossgiel. I was struck in him with the earliest manifestation of perfect instinct I ever saw in collies. It was a little rough-haired colley pup, whose mother belonged to a man who was travelling. As she littered at our place he was going to destroy the pups, but fortunately there was another colley suckling some at the same time, and I made her undertake the office of foster-mother for three by force. I held her down in spite of her resistance while the little fellows I had selected made a meal, and at the end of some days she did not know the strangers from her own, and brought them up together. I kept the most promising one for myself, and named him Bo'son. He was only two months old when I took him with me to Strathavon, and until then he had never beheld a sheep at close quarters. For three or four days I kept him tied up close to my tent, but on the fourth he got away and followed me and my big dog Sancho down to the gate of the paddock where I had just driven about one hundred and fifty rams. On reaching them I found I had left my tools for mending wire fencing behind me, and as I rode back Sancho came with me, for there was no need to fear they would stray far, being slow and steady in their ways, and also somewhat advanced in age. I had not noticed that Bo'son remained behind. On returning in a few minutes I saw, to my surprise, that the rams had not spread out to feed, but were bunched up together in a close mass, and that the outer ones were following the motions of something which I could not see, but which they evidently feared. I reined in my horse, waved back Sancho, and watched. Presently I saw woolly little Bo'son, who certainly was no bigger than the head of the least of them, paddling round and round the circle in a quiet, determined, and business-like manner. I remained motionless and watched to see whether he was doing it by accident; but no, he made his rounds again and again, and as he did so the huge-horned rams followed him with their eyes. It was with much difficulty that I enticed him home, and from his air I have no doubt he would have gone on circling his self-imposed charge until his legs failed him from fatigue. By the time I left Mossgiel he was a very promising sheep-dog.

Sancho, of whom I have spoken, was a large smooth-haired Tasmanian, and the best animal to handle a flock numbering tens of thousands that I ever saw. Yet when I first owned him he had more pleasure in chasing a low-flying crow than in doing his

duty, and it cost me some trouble and him some suffering before I broke him of an unworkmanlike habit due to his former training. He had worked for two years near a well, from which water was drawn in the hot season for the sheep, and to the troughs came not only these, but innumerable crows from many miles round. The men engaged in raising water encouraged Sancho to drive them away and, as one of them, who afterwards worked where I was, told me, he would race up and down for hours at a time while the miserable crows tried in vain to get a drink. Old Veale too pretended that he knew what the birds said about it, and he translated their melancholy cawing into " O-o-h, Sancho-o-o, you wretched dawg," with a long nasal crow-like twang at the end which made Sancho prick up his ears when he heard him relate it. But when I had finished with him he would actually look the other way if a crow flew by, and pretend to be violently anxious to scare anything else in the world. For he was as frightened of my whip as the sheep were of him, and he had reason while they had none.

But I own I had almost enough of sheep while at Mossgiel. How I ever took to them again when I went to Texas I cannot tell. They are the stupidest creatures in all creation, especially when one has to herd them. Fortunately in Australia I had little of that.

One may perhaps make out, by special pleading, that horses and dogs are astonishingly intelligent, but no one can convince a man who has herded sheep, and seen them exhibit their foolishness in a thousand ways, that they are anything but semi-idiotic, although to an outsider without responsibility their obstinacy and obtuseness may be merely farcical. Take this American experience as an example.

Remembering how they served me when I was charged with seeing to their safety and general well-being, I sometimes laugh, but at the time I generally swore. One would think that a ewe who had been the mother of a lamb for several years in succession would at last learn that man was not blood-thirstily desirous of destroying its last acquisition in the shape of offspring, but nevertheless an ancient ewe is as foolish as her grand-daughter, showing the most visible anxiety on one's approach, even when the herder comes to assist her in her trouble. The lambing season is at all times a period of toil and care in a country where the flocks are herded by day and night on account of wild dogs or coyotés; but if the ewes showed the least spark of reason, that would lighten more than half one's burdens. Let me give an illustration, and say that I have a dozen ewes, with offspring from a few hours to a day old, which I must put by themselves. I have made the flock travel during the day, so that their little corral is now no more than half a mile off. Meantime the sun is sinking over the brow of a westward hill, and in less than an hour it will be dark. Surely, a novice would say, it cannot take more than a few minutes to put these in yonder corral, which seems but a step across the plain. Wait, my young friend, and see.

I am on horseback, and have my long stock whip. I go carefully through the flock, slowly drive the mothers out, and gather my twenty-four in one group. I put their heads in the right direction, and move behind them in a quiet walk.

But some of them gaze longingly after those who are not yet mothers, and quietly edge off to the right. I intercept them cautiously. Now that ewe on the left has her head where her tail ought to be, and her lamb totters after her. When I have turned her, those on the right have reversed front again, so I go back a little more quickly. With a sudden jump the hindmost ewe goes on, frightens her nearest neighbour, the last lamb is left alone, and the next one has a ewe by its side which is not its mother. Now the result of this manœuvre is very complex, and not to be disposed of in a few words. The deserted lamb bleats loudly and laments, whereon all the ewes turn round hurriedly in great anxiety, except perhaps the real mother, who is content for a moment with her neighbour's offspring. Perhaps two or three run back a little way, and then their lambs cry out for them to return. By and by the ewe who has the little stranger by her side turns to smell it, and for a moment looks suspicious. When a second sniff has converted her dread suspicion into certainty she butts the poor staggering little wretch over, and scurries fearfully from one to the other, knocking half of them down when she is sure they are not hers. By this time she is at the head of the band, and the horrible thought strikes her that she must have left her lamb with the main flock. She is off like lightning, and so am I, being lucky if I stop and turn her. When I do get her back the others are carefully retracing their steps;

while the deserted lamb, being sure that every sheep it sees is its parent, tries to obtain milk on the strength of the relationship. By the time it has been knocked down half a dozen times the mother comes up at a run, there is a bleat and a baa, and momentary content. I turn them and begin again, being a little heated in temper. I crack my whip softly, and then louder as I move on. Suddenly a lamb, probably the very youngest, is struck with the evident belief that my horse is its mother, and tries to get under his hoofs. I stop until the deserted parent comes and persuades it that a horse after all is not a sheep. When that is settled, and the lamb has taken a little milk to make quite sure, I move on again. Alas! I come a little too close, and a ewe who is smitten with sudden intense hunger and the apparent desire to eradicate one particular knot of grass, does not see me until I am right over her. In a moment she frightens all the rest, the big sheep are together, and the lambs by themselves. Then what a Babel! I have to stop two or three who break out to go to the main body, now some distance away, and then the lambs come to the conclusion that one ewe in particular is responsible for them all, while she is perversely inclined to believe that I have stolen her peculiar and natural property. The other agonized mothers hurry up and dash into the bleating band, smell and butt over one after the other in frantic anxiety, and then subside into their customary demeanour as each finds her own. There is peace once more; but by this time the sun has disappeared, the shadows lengthen rapidly over the dusty plain, and the corral is nearly as far off as it was at first.

What next, then? Why, this, that one lamb declines, poor tired little wretch, to go further on any pursuasion. So I dismount, and lift it up very slowly, while the wild-eyed mother watches every motion I make. I walk on, but before I have got a yard the ewe runs madly after the rest, looking for the very lamb she saw me lift, and her baaing sorrow would make any one else but a sheep-herder pity her. After some ineffectual sniffs, which the other ewes resent, she too thinks that her lamb has returned to the main flock in some miraculous manner, although she ought to know that it cannot move at all. I have to put it down, mount in hot haste, and do another fiery gallop. Then the same thing occurs again, but I am more cruelly careful this time, and pinch the lamb every few yards to make it bleat. The mother runs up and down wildly, but comes to smell it as I stop and hold it out at arm's length. Then she backs, and after another step or two I have to repeat the holding out and pinching, while on both sides of me the others are trying to return. At last I have to put it down and get them together again, with the inevitable result that they all lose their lambs once more, and unanimously resume their sniffing, butting over, and wild rushes, just as if it was the first time it had ever happened. And it is nearly dark by the time we reach the corral. When we do, all the ewes get in while the lambs stay out. On getting the lambs in, the ewes are out. When I think I am on the point of getting them all in one ewe will stay out with the wrong lamb, whom she knocks sprawling. Then she rushes half a dozen times round the corral without seeing the entrance. Meanwhile the lamb finds its mother with the fence in between, and is making great efforts to get through a hole much too small for it, while the mother eyes it from within in the last stage of fear. If I finally can leave them by the time the light of day has quite faded and supper is finished at the camp or home ranch, I am lucky. And this is repeated often and often, until the lambs know their mothers well and the sheep have become accustomed to be nightly corralled.

It may perhaps throw some light on the obscure causes of the stupidity of sheep to see them fight as I often did in the Mossgiel yards. To watch two rams engage in a duel, which they do in a most gentlemanly manner, as if it were as much a matter of etiquette as an engagement with swords in the environs of Paris, is better than most farces nowadays. Perhaps there are some ten or twenty rams in a yard or corral, and presently two put their heads together. Probably they are having a conversation, and in it some debatable matter crops up, for one shakes his head impatiently as if doubting the word of his interlocutor. The insulted ram looks up, advances a step or two, and they rattle their horns together. Instantly all the other gentlemen gather round as the two intending combatants march backwards step by step with an admirable slowness and deliberation. They are the two knights at the ends of the lists. There is an instant's pause, and then they hurl themselves violently forward to meet forehead to forehead with a shock that ought to break their skulls. Then the solemn backward march recommences, the pause is made, and the two belligerents leap at each other once more, and the terrible thud is heard again. Sometimes they run ten courses before one turns dizzy and declines the battle, but oftener five or six blows make the thinner-skulled turn away, to be contemptuously hustled in the rear by the conqueror. Occasionally the sight of one set of duellists inspires the unoccupied lookers-on with a noble ardour, and couple after couple join in to march backwards side by side, and rush forward in line to meet the opposing forces. It seems to me that there is more interest in this than the mere farce of the display. However such a habit arose, it can hardly now be advantageous to the species, and must tend to lower them in the scale of intellect; for while the thickest-skulled remain lords, those with the most room for brains often get their craniums cracked with fatal results. This may help to explain the very uncommon idiocy of domesticated sheep, just as the duello among the Australian blackfellows may throw light on the dull, thick-headedness of some of the native humans in that country. For their favourite method of duelling—at least it was that of which I heard most—is to take two clubs, and having drawn lots in some manner for the first blow, to strike the loser on the head, as he bends down, with the utmost force possible. If that blow is not decisive—and it is not always so—it is the turn of the other man to do his best, and so on until a skull is cracked or its owner rendered insensible. It would be harder to find a nearer parallel to the duel of the rams, except perhaps the butting of fighting negroes.

It was at Strathavon, in this land of sheep, that I first learnt to cook with any degree of skill and certainty. Old Veale taught me to make bread in the proper way. I could even now set "a sponge." I made the yeast from hops which were part of my rations. I even manufactured sugar cakes, called in the bush, "brownies," which were quite eatable. As curry-powder was one of our luxuries, a dish of curry sometimes relieved the usual chop. The Australian bustards, known vulgarly as turkeys, are very plentiful on the saltbush plains, and we often shot them. As the weather grew intensely hot, most of our mutton was salted. We could only have one meal of fresh meat; for though the sheep was killed at midnight it would be bad by dawn in the worst weather. Still salt mutton is not so disagreeable as it may sound to those who have not tried it, and with good bread instead of the uncivilized "damper," or cake of unleavened flour, baked in the ashes, we thought we had very good "tucker." Sometimes I cooked for three or four without much discontent on the part of any temporary guests. I began to get proud. Most boundary riders content themselves with the least possible amount of cooking, "flap-jacks" and "johnny-cakes" are the staple of their indigestible diet. One of the slang names given to boundary riders at Mossgiel was "johnny-cake disturbers." Many of them said it was no use cooking, for some other man would come along when they were away and eat everything up. It certainly is annoying to come home and find the last two loaves gone, eaten by a couple of one's hungry mates who know what man makes bread, and what man contents himself with flap-jacks. Of course cooking well was really little more than a device to fill up my time. After reading a novel fourteen times it palls on the mind; there is a lack of freshness about it. And in making bread there was still an uncertain *dénoûment*.

But as it drew on towards the summer I began to have less time to cook and more to do with the sheep. Fortunately there was plenty of water in the paddocks or I should have had to teach them where to find it. For when the water-holes, or as they call them in that part of Australia, cooliman holes, gave out, it was necessary to resort to the wells, such as the one where Sancho learnt his bad and unbusiness-like habit of crow-hunting. If sheep are left alone in a paddock without water they travel up the wind until they come to a fence. There they remain until they die. At one boundary of my Long Clump Paddock I rode over the skeletons of five thousand who had thus quietly died of thirst. But now it grew on towards shearing time. The shearers from the north began to come south, as they "cut out" the sheds nearer the Tropic of Capricorn. As ours was a big clip they waited for the shearing. Webster made an attempt to reduce the price per hundred. The usual rate was then a pound, the men finding themselves. As it is a very poor Australian shearer who cannot get through more than a hundred a day, the men made good wages. Webster offered seventeen-and-sixpence, and on these terms got a number of men together who camped in and about the shearers' hut. He supplied them with a certain quantity of provisions. But when the gathering grew sufficient to begin work, there was discontent. They demanded the pound. It was refused, and the men rolled up their blankets. I happened to be in at the home station that day, having brought up ten thousand sheep. About two in the afternoon we saw a long procession of horsemen coming from the direction of the woolshed. They were in regular order, marching two abreast, and numbering about a hundred. Behind them came the rouse-abouts, men on foot mostly, those who would have picked up and tied the fleeces, handed the tar to put on cuts, or worked in the yards.

At the head of them all was a man in a red shirt, said to have been a Garibaldian. He was the leader.

They filed slowly through the gate, came to the front of the house, and wheeled into a long line. Then at the signal given by the leader, who called out " Three groans for Mossgiel ! " three groans were given. This was followed by three cheers for Tarrawonga at which station the pound per hundred was given. The boss did not show up, receiving his groans without remonstrance. Then the men jumped off their horses ; and, letting them go, came up to the men's hut where we were standing. Quite unjustifiably, as I now think, seeing they had agreed to take the half-crown less, we were quite in sympathy with them. Without asking leave they cleaned out the kitchen of any eatables and gradually dispersed, mostly going south to Mossgiel township, where a very large proportion got drunk.

This incident was known for a long time as the Great Mossgiel Roll Up. It put the shearing back for a week or two, and it was found necessary to give the pound after all. And the new men had it all their own way. Once when I brought a mob of sheep into the shearing yards from Strathavon, I walked through the shed and heard the superintendent say to one man, " You are putting these out much too rough." The shearer replied coolly, " You'll have them a deal rougher yet ! " If he had been sacked all the rest would have gone with him.

I was now very hard at it mustering in my paddocks. It is not altogether an easy thing to take all the sheep out of a hundred square miles of country, but with five men we usually made a clean sweep of it. On entering the gate we spread out in a line. As I had not very good sight, but was usually as well mounted as the overseer himself, I generally took the fence, going near enough to see that there were no sheep between it and me. If I went to the left I drove all I found over to my right, going all the time at a canter or gallop, until they were taken by the next to me, who kept them in sight. Driving them towards the centre of the paddock his neighbour controlled them. Thus by the time I had passed three out of the four fences we began to close down on the entire mob. Then I could slacken speed, and the long, slow driving on the plains began.

Much as I had admired the thick wooded hills of the Murray, the little river flats, the glory of the golden wattle, and the bright river itself, by slow degrees I came to love more the wide sunburnt plains across which one could gallop at ease in the large freedom of a distant horizon. The Murray country was beautiful and harmonious, but its beauty was broadly marked, its harmony easy to resolve. The plains were subtler, and in the fine distinctions of their music almost unisonic. Only by slow degrees I saw the infinite variety of the unit. As a single note is made up of the pure tone, the overtones and harmonics, so it is with the plains. They seem one, but in nature there is no absolute indivisibility ; with knowledge comes deeper knowledge still. After a great flat plain where a pile of wind-drifted sand is a far landmark, the sea, save in its wilder hours, is monotonous ; after the level land whose horizon is blurred with vapour and set very far off, the sea's round line is restricted. And in mountains, by a curious suggestion of a prison, by the inability to see beyond near barriers, one chokes as for want of air. But the plains are free, the winds unchecked, one looks afar and rides with that same ease of thought given to a man who lives not from day to day, but is set towards some distant goal. If, as has been well suggested by a friend of mine, much of the mysterious attraction of the plain is due to a sudden reversion to the nomadic period of our race's history, some of it is, I think, to be found in this freeing of the will. The mountain path is like civilization, we are not only hemmed in, but we are cursed with the constant necessity for watchfulness, we have continually to shift our course, we compromise with a straight line, we are slaves to a zigzag, we have to think. But on the plains I could live and breathe, could see the end and attain it. I could travel by night, and gallop under the stars.

In those days it was breakfast at the earliest dawn. We were on horseback while the air was still a little fresh, for when I brought up the horses from the small horse paddock I often hunted for them in comparative darkness. It was a great rush to gather the mob, but then Sancho came in useful. Few people in this country have ever seen 20,000 sheep together, and can scarcely imagine what a space of country they cover when they are being slowly driven along at a rate which permits them to feed. Yet my dog Sancho would handle so many with the greatest ease; indeed, the more there were the better he seemed pleased. As a matter of fact, I must acknowledge he was not much good with a very small number. But when I was riding on an endless plain, with the mob spreading out two miles, he would watch for me to wave my hand when all shouting was useless by distance. When he was so far off that I could not distinguish him, I knew well that he was looking out for the signal of a fluttering handkerchief to the right or left, and that he could discern a different motion which meant "that would do." When the flock was set in the right direction, he would make a long bend to come to me, and without any orders keep each wing up, first going half a mile to the left, and then as far to the right.

When the weather was very hot, as it was now, we had to treat our dogs very carefully. They were always fed at night, being allowed to eat as much meat as they could consume, but they never had anything in the morning. If by accident they found enough to gorge themselves on, they did no work; it was impossible to urge them to it, even with a stock-whip. Perhaps at lunch time we could give them a bite of what we carried for ourselves, but it was always very little.

There is one thing that colonial shepherds much dislike when there is going to be a big muster, and that is rain. Though the next day may be fiercely bright, and most of the plain dry enough to be dusty a few hours after dawn, the water will lie for some time in the pools. As sheep work is thirsty work, the dogs rush into these water holes, and drink every time they come across one. Then they come out on the parching ground, and after a while their paws will crack, unless in very good condition. It is no good ordering the dog not to drink, he thinks that does not come in the orders which he is bound to obey. Consequently they often get lame. At night time I used always to examine my dog's feet for these cracks, or for thorns. Fortunately there are no prickly pears in Australia, or the collies would have a bad time of it. Perhaps the prevalence of these pests in America has prevented the common use of dogs in herding.

But gradually the year's great work got done. With a hundred men shearing a hundred a day, and some shearing a hundred and eighty, even two hundred thousand sheep are soon disposed of, and we began to settle down as the weather grew to summer heat. The pressed bales of wool went down the country to Deniliquin in horse and bullock waggons, for the railroad then came no further north I was almost idle once more, and began to regret the change of sometimes sleeping at the shearing-shed, where there were so many men to talk to. If one wanted it there was plenty of gambling going, if not we could sit at the long table and tell stories. The cook for the shearers, a big handsome ne'er-do-well from Dublin, with a queer history, was as good a *raconteur* as a cook. And it takes good cooking to satisfy shearers who pay for their own food. Now I had nothing to do but loaf my usual thirty-five miles a day, being intensely glad if I chanced at the farthest fence to see a boundary rider belonging to the next station. For then we smoked a pipe together and exchanged what news we had, or swapped experiences and life histories. I began at last to think of England again. Australia so far had been to me as a jam-pot is to a fly; the more I tried to get out the further I got in. If I stayed long enough I should come out at the Gulf of Carpentaria. And presently I at last got the chance of going somewhere else. It happened through a cow. I was sent in to Mossgiel to bring out one with her calf. I stayed at the home-station all night, and rose betimes to do what turned out to me my last day's work in that country. Perhaps that is why the day remains with me so strongly. I can see it now as plainly as I saw it then.

It was midsummer, and a clear blue sky was overhead. Under the sun the long brown plains ran to all points of the compass, and, covered with salt and cotton bush, which the hungry sheep had now left leafless and barren, disappeared at the far horizon without the sign of a single hill or even of rising ground. The landmarks of that vast stretch of country without permanent water, were no more than a few isolated clumps of dwarf box-trees, which stood out in the distance like pillars to be seen from afar, or rather like low clouds, for they showed dissevered from the soil, which was then parched and brown by three months of unconcealed and constant sun. Beyond the last faint clump lay Strathavon. It was but fourteen miles and I had all day before me. When, therefore, I mounted my horse after our early breakfast, I considered that I had no more than a fairly easy and comfortable day's work. But I reckoned without my host, and without the wire fences which cut the whole country into squares, and without my horse, an animal untrained to run stock, which I never rode if I could help myself, for he had neither the alertness of intellect nor the quickness of eye and foot necessary for such work. But surely, I said, with only a cow and calf, neither of which was wild, I might manage to make him do. I uncoiled my fifteen-foot stock-whip, cracked it complacently, and started on my journey.

At first my main charge showed no recalcitrance, and, having the whole day before me, I was in no hurry as I lounged easily in my comfortable saddle, and looked across the long plain towards distant Strathavon, directing my way first of all towards the Five Mile Clump. We came to a gate, and passing through it entered a smaller paddock some four miles square. Here the road ran by the side of the fence, which was of wire, and a little more than three feet high, and as my own chief work at this time of the year was once more to look after similar fences, I cast my eye on it every now and again to envy the little trouble it gave the home station boundary rider. For it certainly required little attention, being a strong new fence, well strained up, and without a single bad wire in it, while day by day my own were broken by kangaroos or emus. I did not then think how I should curse those same inoffensive wire threads before I had passed through the paddock they bounded on the northern side, but presently my troubles began, for the cow commenced to show unequivocal signs of a decided disinclination to go any farther as soon as she saw that I was bent upon taking her away from her accustomed pastures and former companions. She lagged so that I was compelled to swing my whip and drop it lightly about her hind quarters until she moved at a more reasonable pace. But this was only the very first of her manœuvres, and much the simplest; the next thing was to drift away from her calf, who apparently had been previously instructed as to the course he was to pursue in such circumstances, for he showed no eagerness to follow in her wake. Then, while I was driving one, the other turned back towards Mossgiel, moving in a nonchalant manner, as though it were out of no evil motive or even quite unconsciously. After zigzagging across the plain for about half a mile, I grew tired of the persistency they showed, and, putting my horse into a gallop, which he resented by a feeble and futile effort to get rid of me, I drove the two together once more, and hurried their lingering pace a little. We were then rather more than a mile from the gate, and suddenly the cow jumped over the fence into the next paddock.

Now some horses will jump wire, and one at least that I constantly rode at Mossgiel never made any bones about it, not even requiring me to strap it down or put my coat on it to show the exact height plainly, but I knew from previous experience that the roan brute I was then blessed with could by no earthly means be persuaded to face it, and therefore I dismounted, climbed the fence, and spent ten hot minutes in vainly endeavouring to make the cow return to her offspring, who in the meantime was slowly wandering back the way we had come. But all my efforts were useless ; she eluded me in every way, and gradually got farther and farther off, until at last I was in a speechless rage and perspiring furiously, for in the summer season of Australia the heat is intense, even an hour or two after sunrise. So I returned panting, crossed the fence, mounted my horse, and galloped right back to the gate.

It may be asked why I did not cut the wires and go through, but I think I can offer enough evidence to prove that I was not quite a fool in acting as I did. In the first place, the fence was new, and I might well have got into trouble about it. In the second, I had nothing to cut it with. In the third, being without my wire tools, I could not have mended it again, and as there were sheep on both sides, close at hand, who might have got mixed if I had found a way to cut it and then left it, that would be another excuse, if any were needed after the two I have given.

When the cow caught sight of me coming up the fence on the same side as herself, she instantly crossed it once more and rejoined her calf, who by this time had accomplished about a quarter of a mile on the return journey. I dismounted, drove them well out into the paddock, and then rode back again. That made a four-mile ride for nothing, but I thought little of that when on coming back I found the cow so close to the fence that, in spite of all my efforts, she jumped it once again. It almost makes me angry to think of it now, but then! I was furiously determined not to go back again, so I wasted half an hour in trying to make my horse jump the fence. I strapped it down with a stirrup leather until it was barely two feet high; I put my coat on it to make it plain; but the only result of all my trouble was increased perspiration and loss of temper, as I divided my growing wrath between the cow and my mount, for he was obstinacy itself upon the point that wire was wire even with a coat upon it, and a dangerous thing to have anything to do with.

I took at last to considering whether I could not

hit upon some more subtle means of gaining my end, and finally I thought that if I were to go on driving the calf, its mother might follow me on the other side. I tried it, but apparently her maternal affection was not so strong as her desire for the old pasture, for she began to graze towards Mossgiel just as placidly as if her offspring were weaned, and had become quite indifferent to her. Then, on finding this fail, I endeavoured to make the calf cross the fence, but as that did not succeed, I myself went over once more, and again chased the mother on foot. In the end I had to give it up, and ride that terrible two miles again. This time I drove her and the calf fully half a mile into the paddock, and fortunately when I returned I found her still on the right side of the fence. I hoped that she was satisfied with the diversion that she had had, but no—the two recommenced the lagging and separation trick, and so well did it succeed, that it took me about two hours to drive them two miles. By that time we were nearing the gate which led into the big paddock, on the far side of which lay our destination, Strathavon. Unfortunately, this same gate was in the corner of the paddock we were in, and I was perforce obliged to take her near the fence, which she had already jumped twice. I came close to it again with fear and trembling, and my worst fears were realized, for no sooner did she see it within a hundred yards than she rushed at it, and was over once more. If I had been mounted on any kind of a stock horse, or even an apology for one, it would never have happened, but the blundering brute I rode could not turn until I lugged his head round by force, and he always overshot his mark like an ill-handled boat trying to pick up moorings. I confess to being nearly heart-broken, and quite past swearing, for I was hoarse already, so I sat for a while in despair to take in the situation, which was now worse than ever. The gate behind us which I had used twice was four miles away, and the one in front— the one at least which led into the paddock she now occupied in triumph—more than two. However, there was nothing else for it, and to that gate I went. This means that I rode nearly five miles to reach her. After sending her over with a few extra whipmarks upon her hide, I tried to drive them on foot the remaining distance to the gate leading into Strathavon paddock, but after running until I was tired I had to ride back after all. That made another five miles, and my horse, who had now gone more than sixteen unexpected miles, began to show signs of fatigue. I wondered anxiously what was going to happen—indeed, I made up my mind to leave her if she crossed those wires again, and kept as much as possible between her and the fence. But this time, and at last, I actually got her through the gate, and there were no more to pass. I thought all my troubles were over, since the road went near no fences, although I had still about nine miles to go under the burning sun.

Time passed, and it was now close upon four o'clock, although we were still about five miles from Strathavon, whose corrugated iron roof I could just see across the level ground. I tried to rouse up the failing energies of my horse, but found him almost dead-beat. Could I have incited him by any means to gallop I would have put the cow into the same pace, which, by the way, should never be done with a milker; but, try as I would, I could not get him to follow her turnings, which even now showed the same obstinate bent towards Mossgiel they had done when she first discovered that I intended

taking her away from home. At last we came to a pool, or water-hole, about three feet six inches deep and some forty feet across, and into this she plunged. I went in and she came out, I came out and she went in, like the man and woman in the old-fashioned country predictor of coming weather, and neither by rein nor whip nor spur could I get my jaded horse to exhibit sufficient energy to eject her and keep her ejected. It was a case of merely formal eviction. Finally I grew so wrathful that I struck my horse and broke my stock-whip handle in two pieces, and thus rendered it entirely useless as a means of persuasion. That was the last straw, and the back of my persistence broke. After gazing speechlessly at the whole earth and sky for some *deus ex machinâ* who came not, I turned towards Strathavon, leaving the cow in the pool, but meditating as I went along upon the awful surprise I should give her when I returned. When I reached home I did what I might have done at first—rode into the paddock, ran up to the horses, selected a mare called Beeswing, the quickest animal after cattle of any kind on the whole station, put my saddle on her, and after mending my whip went back at a hard gallop, to find the cow still complacently cooling herself in the water. She seemed to look at me with an air of contempt, thinking herself mistress of the entire situation, but she reckoned without her host, being ignorant that my bright bay mare was not cut after the pattern of the roan. I wasted no time, but drove straight at the pool, and taking off from a bank about two feet above the water-level, landed seven yards off with a tremendous splash and a loud yell close by her side. As I struck the water my renewed whip struck her, and made her move with far more alacrity than she had displayed at any time during that tiring and most ridiculous day. In a single moment I had the cow and calf together, and headed them for home. There was never any need to tell that mare what to do—indeed, I could actually have trusted her to accomplish her work without a bridle, for she was first on one side and then on the other, following every motion made, while my stock-whip swung through the dusty air and cracked like rifle shots behind them as they rushed bewildered and terror-stricken at the sudden alteration in affairs through the dry salt bush straight for Strathavon. I know that I drove them harder than I should have done, but I really think that that cow earned, fairly earned, the treat she got and the painful lesson I taught her. At the same time I know that I too learnt a lesson, and that was, never to ride when it can be helped after obstinate or wild cattle upon a horse which has neither knowledge nor instinctive aptitude for his arduous and peculiar business.

But though that was the end of the day's business for the cow, it was not for me. The overseer came down to the yard, and looking at the mother and calf, told me sharply I had driven them too hard. I replied I knew that very well, and that if I had to drive that cow again I would kill her. I was very hot and tired and angry. He replied in a way I did not admire, so I told him that he could milk her in the morning if he liked, that I would take nothing in the shape of reproof from him, and that I should go to Mossgiel next day. We had no more words, but by ten o'clock on that day I received my cheque at the home station, and with about forty pounds in my pocket set my face to the south.

CHAPTER XII.

HUNGER AT BULLIGAL CREEKS.

I own to having experienced an intense repugnance to walking down to Deniliquin or even to Hay on the Murrumbidgee. After so many months of fairly living on horseback I had become like the typical colonial of the bush who will walk two miles to catch a horse to go one. To Bulligal, on the Lachlan, our nearest town, was nearly seventy miles; thence to Hay, on the Murrumbidgee, across the One Tree Plain, about fifty; and thence again over the Old Man Plain to Deniliquin, where I could take the railroad, not less than ninety—in all, two hundred and ten miles, which, even if I made no halts, would take me ten days' travel. The prospect was not pleasant to me, for, moreover, the roads were almost axle-deep in dust, while the skies rivalled those of the last burning Christmas which I had passed at Mahonga. It was a relief to find that there was a team going to Hay with a load of sheepskins, and I gladly accepted the driver's offer to take me with him on condition of my helping to harness the horses and to cook. I had no pleasure in "humping my swag," and I threw my blankets on his load.

That night we camped near a tank, and filled all our water-bags and bottles, for we were to drink no more fresh water for three days, being forced to trust to the wells, which were nauseous and brackish to a degree. Our camping-ground was on the open plain, and the mosquitoes were so watchful and numerous, on account of the near water, that I was at last obliged to roll myself completely up in my blankets, and there I lay, sweating and suffocating the whole night through.

When our fresh water was at an end we took a new supply from a well which had all the bad qualities of the most evil spring at Gloucester (in England) and foul bilge-water mixed. I was forced to hold my nose to drink it; but, bad as it tasted, the heat of the day was so tremendous that I was obliged to have recourse to it at exceedingly short intervals, although each time it seemed worse than it was before. For three whole days we had no other, and I was beginning to think that life was not worth living at the price, when Johnstone, the driver, pointed out a little house, or shanty, about a mile in front of us, asking me if I saw it. I answered sulkily enough, but soon altered my tone when he told me that there was real fresh water to be had there, in a big water-hole, or cooliman hole, as we called it in Back Blocks. I walked towards it at a good five miles an hour pace; the last hundred yards I ran;

and then I threw myself down in the mud, and, resting my elbows fairly in it, put my head down and drank like a horse. English people would call it muddy, and complain of its flavour, but it was nectar to me; the sweetest draught I ever swallowed. And I swallowed a good deal!

That was the last day of my suffering for water, but next day suffering of a kind was to come which till that time I had known very little of. It was starvation, and I believe from my experience then that few people know what the word means better than I do.

At sundown we camped right in the middle of the Bulligal Creeks, a network of streams which were either quite dry or running feebly with a small thread of water at the bottom of their deep, wide beds. After crossing two of them, we unharnessed the horses, for there was some grass there of a distinct green, quite unmistakable for old hay or chips, and the driver wanted to give his horses the benefit of the fresh feed. After eating supper, I called Johnstone's attention to the fact that there was no more "tucker," or food. That was all right, he said; to-morrow we should be in Bulligal. But he reckoned without his host, and we did *not* see Bulligal on the morrow. We had not crossed all the creeks as we should have done.

The spot we had chosen for our camping-ground was pleasant enough, having sufficient of freshness and greenery about it after our sixty miles of shadowless, sandy journeying to make it welcome, to my eyes at least. The trees were no longer dwarf boxes, but gums of a more reasonable stature, and standing closely together they were not so dusty and full of grime as their sparse and thin congeners of the outer plains. Here, too, was a little water, and a few birds chattered and screamed among the branches. It did not occur to either of us that they were feathered barometers and foresaw a change in the weather, nor when I rolled myself in my blankets and stared at the stars, as I smoked my last goodnight pipe, did I think that their sharper and more brilliant appearance betokened rain in the near future. Both of us, indeed, lay down in the open, disdaining the cover of the waggon, and expecting anything rather than a wet night. We easily got to sleep, for the mosquitoes were fortunately few, the surface of water for their hatching being so small. My companion put his head under his blanket, but I kept mine outside, and was consequently roused first, when just about midnight something wet fell on my face. I started, thinking that perhaps one of our horses was standing over me, and had dropped some foam as he chewed greener grass than he had lately been accustomed to; but when I raised myself upon my elbow, I saw that it was darker than it should be, that there was a lively wind blowing, and that the sky was covered with a dense mass of clouds. Before I could move the deluge commenced, and ere I could bundle my blankets together I was wet through. Johnstone did

not need calling, and in a few seconds we were crouching under the bed of the waggon, cursing and grumbling in a duet. We spread our blankets again and tried to get to sleep.

The rain came down as if it was in a hurry, for none had fallen for four months, and as if it was trying to make up for lost time. In half an hour we heard the rush of water in the creeks above the ceaseless roar of the rain, and then, although we seemed to be in a fairly high position, the water began to encroach upon us on all sides, the splashes moistened us all over, and by the morning we were lying in a pool of mud, which stuck upon our blankets in cakes. At daylight I rose, and putting one of mine round me I went out to inspect the creeks, for I began to think we were in a "tight place," as they say in America. I was right enough, for, behind and before us, they were running full to the very banks, covered with drift wood and foam, roaring as they rushed to the Lachlan. The smallest was twenty feet wide, and from what we had seen of them when they were empty, I knew that they must at least be twelve feet deep. The rain did not cease, indeed it scarcely lessened in intensity, and the prospect before us was not encouraging, for neither horse nor man could ford such streams.

It was time for breakfast, and there was none to be had. It rained and it was noon, but the dinner was as unsubstantial as the breakfast, and there was no hope of supper. I had never at that time been really hungry. It is true that on my journey from Forbes to Mossgiel I had lived for three days on jam and pancakes, which began to pall on me after a few meals ; but that was not true hunger, although I and Charlie did gorge ourselves so ravenously on that salted mutton when we obtained meat at last. But now I really began to starve, and before I saw Bulligal, I could have passed an examination on the symptoms and progress of that peculiarly distressing complaint.

A little after noon it almost ceased to rain, but the creeks showed no sign of lessening, in spite of the enormous volume of water they carried at the rate of three or four miles an hour. Still we knew that they would soon go down, if the rain did not continue, and we hoped that it would not. But the sky was still threatening, and it came on to rain in the evening as hard as ever. By this time we had been without food twenty-four hours, and I began to feel so very hollow and ill at ease, that I contemplated swimming the creeks. On inspecting them carefully however, I came to the conclusion I was much safer where I was, and I went to my wet and muddy blankets to sleep instead of eating.

In the morning the rain ceased for a while, the sun came out, and then it again commenced pouring. The trees about us looked beautiful and fresh, the grass began to spring, and by the time I had done without another three meals, there was a pleasantly perceptible tint of verdure on spots which had been bare for three months. This second day of fasting was extremely painful, for I had terrible gnawing pains in the stomach which came and went, returning with fresh force, which at times bent me nearly double. For six months at least I had been accustomed to plentiful and regular meals, and now I paid an extra penalty for my former comfort. I have starved since then, but not quite so systematically, and it is a fact that those who eat at uncertain intervals do not suffer from prolonged fasting (up to a certain point, that is) as much as those who live with clockwork regularity.

By evening I was much worse than Johnstone, who, being an older and stronger man than myself, was more enduring than I, whose age was then not quite twenty-one. I went continually to the creek and filled myself with water, which by distending the stomach eased the pain; but the relief was only temporary. Then I turned to tobacco and chewed that, and certainly it was of great assistance to me. I now began to think of the stories I had read of cast-away seamen, and of what they had eaten, and I found out the falsehood of much that I had been told in other days. People say that a hungry man will eat anything eatable, however horrible it may be. I know that he will not always do so, for I actually grew dainty and fastidious. I went several times to the box in which we had kept the food, and on turning out everything I found a little piece of bread, less than two inches square. I had made a great discovery, I thought, but could scarcely make up my mind to share it with my companion. I went through a severe struggle before I came to the conclusion that I ought at least to go halves. But, alas! it was not only mouldy but sour, and when I put my teeth into it, it nearly made me ill. Then I offered the whole piece to Johnstone, but he could not eat it either. So I put it back into the box, visiting it several times in the course of the day, thinking that I was perhaps hungry enough to swallow it at last. But all my attempts to get it down failed, for the smell revolted me, and I absolutely loathed it.

That night, the second without food, was a dreadful one. I kept on dreaming of gorgeous banquets, and of simpler repasts, and in my voracious dreams I had a stomach capacity which would have satisfied a Roman Emperor. For however much I ate, I was still hungry, and hungrier yet. Many times I woke, and groaning savagely, I tightened my belt in more and more, and fell asleep to commence my calenture of Lucullus anew, and with no more satisfaction. As I lay there I seemed to return to Mossgiel, and in my dreams I renewed my old loathed occupation of butcher. I seemed to catch a sheep. I killed and skinned it eagerly, and then cooking it slightly, I swallowed it half-raw in huge gobbets, such as the Cyclops might have savoured. But it was all vanity and emptiness, and I woke again and again unsatisfied and disappointed.

In the morning the pain had passed away, and though I felt ill and very weak, I suffered no extreme anguish. The rain had finally ceased in the night, and the sun shone out as hotly as though there had never been a cloud in the sky. Yet the creeks were much too full to attempt to cross, and though this was the third day of our fasting it had to be endured, for now I had not the strength to swim. Johnstone and I rarely spoke to each other, and sat apart doing nothing, save when we went to the creek and drank. I fancy his sufferings were scarcely comparable with my own, but he bore them with at least equal doggedness, and made no complaint. During this third day I got at times rather light-headed, perhaps partly from my constantly chewing tobacco, which at last threw me into a sort of dull coma, for the nicotine had a much stronger effect than was usual, although it did not make me feel in the least ill. I had not smoked since the second morning, and had no desire for the pipe.

I was in such a state of dreaminess, with so little volition, that the outside world seemed to have a very feeble existence for me. Had nothing happened to rouse me from this comparatively pleasurable state of weakness, I could have been almost content to die. But I certainly was not to die in peace. The sun, which had been fierce and strong all this third day, had hatched millions of mosquitoes, who rose in the evening in swarms, and hung under the trees in black clouds, each composed of tens of thousands. As long as it was still light they did not trouble us much, and their irritating *ping ping* came but seldom, considering their numbers. But as the sun went down, and darkness fell on the earth, they seemed to suddenly smell us out, and came in legions and myriad battalions thirsting for our blood. They hung around us in swarms; they got into my ears, my eyes, and down my neck; they flew up my sleeves, and almost bit me into madness. Our horses stood and stamped and switched themselves with their tails, snorting to blow them out of their nostrils, and rushed through the bush, at last making a charge for the creek, which they swam over, running far out into the plain. As for me, weak as I was, I hunted for damp wood to build smoky fires to drive them away. But still we could not keep them off. It was as if they had sworn to leave no blood in us, and I was in no state to lose much. At last, in desperation, we got our blankets, and lying down to leeward of the fires, we rolled ourselves up tighter and tighter until we were nearly suffocated, for the night was terribly hot, and we were artificially warmed as well. But it was in vain to attempt to get free of them, for they crawled in at every hole and corner of the blankets, and we fought with them all night until early morning. The torment almost made me forget that I was hungry, and the irritation roused me to unnatural exertions. But at dawn weary and exhausted nature could stand it no longer, and I fell into a dead sleep. In a few minutes, doubtless, I was disencumbered of the blankets, and the mosquitoes had their will of me. As I did not at that time wear long boots, they crawled up my legs, and bit me in hundreds of places right to the knees. They got inside my shirt and bit me all over. Where the sun of three fierce summers had burnt me to a deep mahogany colour the bites did not swell and itch, but where the skin was of its natural whiteness I was smarting with countless intolerable lumps. Next day the irritation was so extreme that I scratched myself until the blood ran down to my ankles. It can be imagined what a pleasant one that fourth day of hunger and pain was.

About noon Johnstone, who had been sounding the creeks, announced that they would soon be shallow enough for the waggon to get across. This was joyful news, and shortly after he waded through and drove up the horses. He and I languidly harnessed them and started. We had not gone ten yards before the king bolt of the waggon broke! It was too disappointing, we did not know sufficient bad language to say anything strong enough for the occasion, and were silent. This accident necessitated our unloading the waggon, and though it was easy enough throwing off the bales, when we came to lifting the bed to get the bolt out it was almost too much for us. I was tempted to refuse to try it, but if I did, I should certainly have to walk into Bulligal in my then state of hunger and weakness. Besides, it would be mean to refuse aid to my companion in misfortune, although I was pitiably feeble with the fasting, heat, and profuse perspiration. When we were at last able to reach the bolt, Johnstone put the two pieces into a sack, and mounting a horse, rode off to town to get a new one made, and to procure food.

But I had many hours to wait yet, though he went away a little after noon. When he was out of sight I used my remaining strength to gather a pile of wood, and having lighted a fire to be ready for cooking, I lay down and fell into a broken and uneasy slumber, in which my dreams ran still on eating, and again on eating. Fortunately a breeze sprang up at sundown and drove the mosquitoes away, for if they had been as vicious and countless as on the previous night I believe it would have proved the last straw, and I should have taken leave of my senses. Even as it was, I was on the borders of feverish delirium, and in my dreams passed beyond them. Yet although it was more than four days since I had put anything inside my lips save water and tobacco, I did not feel as intensely hungry as might be imagined. I knew well that my sensations of lightness, hollowness and intense weakness were caused by famine, yet the feeling of acute and eager hunger seemed to have passed away. For I was in the chronic stage, as it were. Doubtless if I had been deprived of food for much longer these pains might have returned in full or redoubled force, but so far I was relieved physically. I have never in all my wanderings come across a man who has absolutely fasted for so long a period as myself, unless perhaps it was the "Man-Eater" about whom I have spoken in another place, but some I have known who were three days with nothing to eat, and our experiences were similar on this point.

As I have said, I slept, and at times I slept soundly, for although I spent some hours of that fearfully long evening in listening for the returning steps of my comrade's horse, and in cursing his delay, when he did actually return he rode to the fire where I was lying, and called me by name before I heard him. He threw me down the bag, which contained, in addition to the new king bolt, some raw beef and bread. I well remembered even then that it was inadvisable to eat in large quantities, but I was so wholly unable to restrain myself that I threw a steak on the hot wood coals, and rending a loaf with my hands, I crammed the bread into my mouth, and then devoured the steak half raw. If what I have read of the evil effects of sudden gorging in famine were always true, I ought to have paid some penalty for my folly, but as it happened, I took no harm from a fairly Gargantuan repast For I ate like an Esquimaux or a Yakut Indian, and rolling myself in my blankets I fell into deep and undisturbed slumber. I had been without food for a hundred and six hours.

In the morning we loaded the bales on the mended waggon, and as Johnstone declined to move that day, for it was Sunday, and the Bulligal Bridge was Puritanically closed to wheel traffic, I shook hands with him and we parted. I walked into town, and that evening camped alone nine miles south of that place on the One Tree Plain. This was an eighteen mile walk, and I think it was no mean feat for anyone to accomplish after the privations which I had endured. My next stage was twenty miles, and by noon on the day following I entered Hay, a ragged, brown, and weary traveller. I was tired of walking, and taking the coach across the Old Man Plain I reached Deniliquin by the next morning, and was in Melbourne early in the afternoon.

In the train I made the acquaintance of a young Frenchman, named Landerer, and we walked through Melbourne together. He had come from a little further north than Mossgiel and was bound home to Paris. We made a curious pair in a civilized city. As a general rule men coming from the bush rig themselves up in new clothes before reaching town. But he and I had made no alteration. Yet compared with me Landerer was respectable. A little ragged, perhaps, and very dusty, that was all. As for me I had scarcely a button anywhere, the lining was gone from my coat and hung in ragged ends out of the sleeves; my wide hat was full of holes; my boots had not been blacked since I bought them. My face was so tanned that even among sailors I looked very dark; the deep red burn ran into a point down to my chest, for my shirt was always wide open; my hands were tinted like old mahogany. On our backs we carried our swags. Such travellers were rare in town. Every one stared at us curiously. The police took a great interest in me. Just at that time the bushranging gang of the Kelly brothers was very hard pressed up in the Wombat Ranges, and it was expected that they would try to leave Australia. So when two policemen asked me carelessly if I had just come to town I knew what they were thinking of. They walked by us for a hundred yards. I conversed carelessly but at last stopped, looked them full in the face, and said, "Come now, I am not in the least like Ned Kelly or any of the gang so far as I know. And if I look a little wild I am not Wild Wright." They laughed and left us. Landerer went to a Swiss *pension*. After staying in Melbourne for a day or two I began to think it time to make my arrangements for going to England.

CHAPTER XIII.

IN THE FOC'SLE.

I HAD made up my mind, even before leaving the Lachlan Back Blocks, to return to the "old country" before the mast, and thus to earn money instead of spending it. Had I been a professional sailor there would have been nothing risky or out of the way in my so doing; but although I knew much more about ships and a sailor's work than most landsmen, I had only been one passage in a sailing vessel, and that in the character of a passenger. During the hundred and two days that it took us from Liverpool to Cape Otway, in the *Seringapatam*, I had, with an eye to future contingencies, learnt the names of all the ropes and gear, their leads and uses, and had so persisted in going aloft that I was at last capable of service there. Hence I considered myself something of a "sailor-man," and thought that with the faculty I have always possessed of learning most simple handiwork at sight, I might easily pass for a trained man, considering that I was yet young, and looked even younger than I was.

My first step was to put up at a sailors' boarding-house in Williamstown, one of the ports of Melbourne, and I went there in a cheap slop rig of seaman's serge, which suited my complexion, burnt to such a dark tint in the New South Wales sun, and my walk, which was a queer compound of a sea roll and a cavalry stride, due to my two years spent almost entirely in the saddle. The boarding-house was one of the very rowdiest and most disreputable places in the town, which could boast no few dens in which a new chum would have hesitated to set his foot.

In this "hotel" there were two doors to the bar, which was backed by a gaudy glass and gaudier bottles of spirits, with piles of cheap cigars in boxes and bundles. The space in front was half choked with barrels, some stowed on their bilges, each of which rocked with an intoxicated seaman or loafer, and some on their chimes, which held spilt beer. Here and there were piles of seamen's bags thrown on the barrels, together with ragged coats discarded on account of the heat or for purposes of personal combat; while the floor was covered with the "doddle" from the bottom of juicy clays, with old cigar-ends, with saliva or beer, and the atmosphere reeked with tobacco fume in conflict with the subtler and more persistent odour of spirits. The customary occupants of this den were certainly admirably placed in such a *milieu*, for few of them were either clean or sober by the hour of noon; while there was a perpetual din of argument, of beery chuckles, of angry oaths, or of violent laughter, which rose and fell but never wholly died away, until the last man was violently ejected at closing-time or dragged out by some more sober companion. I remained in this house seven days, and during that short time I witnessed or took part in eight fights. How many others occurred in my absence I cannot tell; but as a general rule some one or other was adorned by a new bruise or black eye each time I returned from town.

The eating-room in this house was an extraordinary apartment, and deserves more than the few words I can bestow upon it. The rough pine-tables and benches, which had been hacked by generations of boarders with dinner and sheath knives, were securely clamped to the floor, which was only occasionally swept and apparently had never been washed, in order that they might not be broken up and converted into weapons if any general row should arise at meal times. The windows were fixed at least six or seven feet from the floor, and higher still at one end of the room was a strongly-nailed notice, bearing the peremptory legend, " Order *must* be preserved," which sufficiently declared how very liable the peace was to be broken. The meals we got in this charming place were what might have been expected, served as they were on the bare deal with unpolished knives and two pronged forks, with potatoes boiled in their skins in tin dishes, and steaks which the strongest-jawed and most sharp-toothed seaman could scarcely chew, even when impelled by hunger ; while the tea and coffee were infusions of some mysterious herb or berry, which tasted sufficiently like neither to pass, under stress of circumstances, for both. Our waiters were a slatternly girl, and a boy who wiped his hands upon his dirty face as though it were a jack-towel.

I had been accustomed to roughing it in the bush, but this was a trifle rougher than I liked, and I made preparations for getting away. To ship in most ports, at least where seamen are plentiful, a " discharge " from another vessel is usually indispensable. To use the phrase of common domestic service, this paper constitutes a man's "character," and as I of course possessed none, I was obliged to buy a certificate from some one else—a proceeding by which I believe I laid myself open to the charge of a misdemeanour of some kind, punishable by fine and imprisonment. I went to the "runner," who looked up ships for the men in the house or touted for new-comers, and told him that I wanted a vessel for England, offering him at the same time a sovereign if he shipped me within a week. That was sufficient to render him anxious to get me off his hands, and I had no fear that he would not exert himself on my behalf, if I danced attendance on him at the shipping office.

Just at this time there was a feeble sort of strike for higher wages in existence among the "deep-water" sailors of the port. Five pounds a month for able seamen was what captains were giving, and the men wished to obtain six. On my first visit to the office I was accosted by their recognized leader, and by him invested with a small piece of blue ribbon in token that I too was on strike, a proceeding that caused me no small amount of inward amusement, considering that I had no right to call myself a sailor. But I took it seriously, and for some days marched about with a band of about two hundred, sometimes carrying a banner and sometimes simply walking in the ranks, answering with my new friends and fellow-strikers the chaff of the bystanders, who laughed good-humouredly at Jack ashore. Yet the strike was a mere farce; there were too many idle men for it to be sustained, and some were constantly shipping at the ordinary rate. On the fifth day the runner called me in, and I signed, under his own

discharge, which he sold me on our original bargain, as Edward Mitchell, A.B., or able-bodied seaman, in the barque *Wessex*, bound to London. On coming out I was laid hold of, and being asked for what rate of pay I had signed, I said six pounds a month, for if I had not lied in company with the others who had shipped with me, I should have been mauled by the strikers then and there, and have made enemies of my shipmates for the passage home.

That afternoon I devoted to buying what things were necessary, and it was at a scandalous den of thieves that I purchased a big monkey-jacket, that was a regular "Cape Horner," a suit of oilskins, a pair of gum or rubber sea-boots, a sheath-knife, which I still possess and shall keep as a memento of the past, a tin plate, cup, and a knife and fork. The boarding-house keeper, who was as big a ruffian as I have ever foregathered with, and I have known many, looked hard at me as I produced five or six pounds to pay the bill, which was probably no more than 300 per cent. too much, and said earnestly—

"If I had known that you had as much money as that, my boy, you wouldn't have gone out of my house for a while!"

He meant it, and didn't mind my knowing that he did. I smiled amicably.

"Thank you," I said; "but I didn't mean you to know. However that's the lot, and now I'm nearly dead broke. So there's no more to be got out of me."

This was not true, for I still had twenty pounds in my belt; but I was scarcely fool enough to let him know that, for I should most assuredly have been drugged and robbed that very night. Yet in spite of his ignorance I was glad to get on board the *Wessex*, a barque of rather more than a thousand tons, at five o'clock the next morning.

I confess to feeling somewhat scared about the step I had taken. It is a serious thing to profess one's self an able seaman on board a vessel about to make a long passage. On land any obvious incapacity to do what is expected only results in being told to go elsewhere; but a man cannot be discharged at sea, and failure to do his duty brings down on him the wrath of the officers, together with the grumbling, and, if they dare, the ill-usage of the crew, who have to make up for his shortcomings. Nevertheless I determined to do my best to be second to none, to learn all that I could, and above all to be very "willing," for that covers a multitude of sins at sea. So if there was anything I could do I jumped to do it; I was first up aloft and the last down, and being always ready to take anything off my next mate's shoulders, and always cheerful, I had my reward.

At ten o'clock we mustered aft, and were put into watches, with the result that I occupied the proud position of "foretopman" in the starboard watch, there being another of the same denomination, a young Dublin fellow, named Jack Reynolds

With him I hastened to make friends, telling him I had not been to sea for a long time, and that the discharge I had shipped under was not mine. He was a good-tempered, easy-going, round-faced man of about twenty-three, and my judgment of confiding in him was not at fault, for he made a regular chum of me, and often saved me from reprimand.

For four days we lay at anchor in Hobson's Bay, off the watering-place called Queenscliffe, waiting for a wind, and during this time I had to keep my eyes open and my wits about me to an extent that almost fatigued me. Every little thing that I saw done, but did not know, I managed to learn; everything I heard I caught up, and I watched every one out of the corners of my eyes. If anything was going on that I was ignorant of, I skulked most skilfully, and made up for it by jumping like a cat to do anything that I understood. Sometimes, however, I got fairly caught, and had to exercise ingenuity which, until it was required, I did not believe I possessed; but day by day my confidence and knowledge grew, until I began to think myself a real seaman and not a mere make-belief.

The *Wessex*, though of such a size, carried no more than six able seamen in each watch, with two boys in mine and an ordinary seaman in the other. Besides these, there was the bo'son, and each watch had a bo'son's mate, who live in the deckhouse. Our foc'sle was forward, and was dark, draughty, and uncomfortable. There were no proper doors to it, and when a heavy sea came over the bulwarks it usually found its way amongst us under the tarpaulin screen which but ineffectually kept out the wind. Our dining-table was the hatch over the fore-peak, where the spare gear was kept, or more frequently our knees, and we sat down on chests, on the deck, or on a low partition which ran fore and aft just where the cable lay when the chain was bent on to the anchors. It was in these quarters that I made a more intimate acquaintance with my shipmates as we grumbled over the quantity or quality of the food, or told strange and surprising adventures of our last ships, which in my case were partly apocryphal, or drawn from the vessel in which I had gone to Australia as a passenger. I even excited envy because my story included the narrative of that outbreak among the Lascars on board the *Seringapatam*, which I have already related.

My mates included an old seaman of sixty, called Mac, who had followed the sea since he was ten, and had become by natural endowment and foremast education a great and admirable liar. His yarns were mostly received with silence, except by Jack Shaw, a discontented old grumbler of a man, who would argue and, if need were, fight about anything. But as these two had tried conclusions in Melbourne in a fight in which Jack had been victorious, Mac only received his contemptuous comments in sulky silence, which lasted until there seemed a reasonable chance of reeling off another stiff yarn, which outdid the last. Shaw and I often bickered, because he knew I carried a "purser's name" (*i.e.* one not my own), and was not quite so experienced a seaman as I should have been. But as he was lame from an old injury to his knee, and I bore no malice, but on the contrary often did things for him, we never really quarrelled. Yet he invented a nickname for me, calling me "Lord Paget," and not content with conferring this brevet nobility upon me, professed to be anxious to reach England in order to see my father arrive with a coach-and-six to bear me to some palatial residence. He took me for a runaway apprentice, and deemed me a marvellously well-educated man when it turned out that I knew enough French to read what was said outside some tinned meats which bore directions for cooking in that language. This indeed was sufficient to make me an authority on anything, and I was frequently appealed to on points of difficulty, such as the relative quantity of ice above and below water in an iceberg. Here, however, my decision was received with scorn, and it was only when I established my dictum by an appeal to a book in our doctor's possession that I recovered and confirmed my authority.

By the time affairs had become as settled as this, we had been at sea for some time, and had experienced a gale far to the south-east of New Zealand in the same latitude where the *Somersetshire* of our line had once been totally dismasted.

The chief mate seemed quite superstitious about the locality, and from his nervousness one might have imagined that he considered this part of the ocean a kind of Quilp's yard, with a gale lurking on one side or the other ready for a spring. It was due more to him than to the captain that we hove the vessel to in only a moderate gale of wind—moderate at least compared with some I have seen before and since—and drifted to leeward for about twelve hours. For my own part I was glad when we were hove to, or running under shortened sail, for then, barring accidents, there was nothing to do, and the watch on deck might retreat to the foc'sle and smoke. Perhaps it is not positive comfort to be idle if all one's clothes are damp, and to sit in a wet shirt with wet oilskins is not wholly cheerful, yet I confess to liking it better than hard work.

On such nights the scene in the dim foc'sle was in its way picturesque. The gale is blowing hard, but everything is made snug, the ropes coiled on their pins, and the " That'll do the watch " of the officer on duty sends both watches below, one for sleep and the other for shelter, until some unwelcome order is bellowed from the poop. In a few moments the port watch are in their bunks, their hanging lamp is extinguished by the last man, while on our side the dim oil burns and swings with the variable roll and pitch of the vessel. It requires some time to discern by its light that the foc'sle is wedge-shaped, and that the bunks line both sides in a double tier. Each of these is about two feet wide and eight inches deep, while there is so little space to spare between the bottom boards and the deck above, that I sometimes bump my head if I am called very unexpectedly. There is no prospect of our being wanted for a while, so taking off my sou'-wester and oilskin coat, I throw myself into my bunk, with my wet sea-boots over the edge, and smoking a short black clay pipe, I look down on the others. Jack Reynolds, my fellow foretop-man, sits on his chest beneath me, with his black painted oilskins shining in the dim light as his hands move slowly about an apparently endless task of making a round sinnet chest-lashing.

In the darkest corner sits little old Mac; I can guess it is he, for his glowing pipe is so low down; and on his own chest is Jack Shaw, mumbling and grumbling as usual while he rubs his left knee. He once fell from a vessel's main royal yard, and struck the side with his leg, going overboard. His companion fell on the deck, and never spoke again. If I turn my head, I see various sea-boots projecting from the other bunks, and on the deck are streams of water, for as she plunges and dives into the head sea, it spurts in through the ill-plugged hawse-pipes, or holes in the bow for the cables, and drips through the cracks of the scuttle or hatchway above us. Every now and again a heavy sea strikes against the bow where I am lying, for we are hove to on the starboard tack, and makes everything shiver and groan; while outside there is a vast and perpetual harmony of stringed instruments, for every stay and shroud sings strange music, and even the braces are bent inward by the wind and tautened like bars. On deck over my head is our lookout man, and I hear his steps as he walks to and fro in the steadier intervals, or his stamps as he tries to restore the circulation in his feet.

It was already March when we rounded the Horn, and very fine it was, with none of the traditional hard weather to make work. The long westerly rollers were unbroken by the steady wind, which allowed us to keep most of the lighter sails set, and would not have prevented us shaking out the royals had not the yards been sent down on deck some time before. We passed far to the south, even of the Diego Ramirez Islands, which sailors, with their extraordinary faculty of mispronunciation, usually call the "Dagarammarines," and had been in the Atlantic forty-eight hours before the fine dry days came to an end. But then a sample of weather fit and appropriate to those latitudes came howling after us.

For nearly three weeks we were in a succession of gales, and it was "Hands shorten sail," and "Hands make sail," alternately with a persistency which almost wore us out, for we were, as is now only too usual, much undermanned; and it still blew hard, even when we shook out a reef or set the topgallant sails above the reefed topsails. Long before this I was able to sit astride the yard and haul out the weather earing myself, and do everything that came to hand, so I considered I had that right to growl which may fairly be thought due to a man who knows his work and is exceedingly uncomfortable. Indeed some home-keeping youth might consider our plight deserved a stronger epithet. For one thing, the foc'sle got more and more leaky; my blankets, by reason of the dripping from the deck above, the perpetually moist air, and the water I was forced to import into my bunk personally, became almost as wet as when I had camped on the Lachlan river in three weeks rain, and one by one my few clothes were soaking as well, for it was impossible to dry them. When I went below, I had to turn into a cold, moist bed, which soon began to steam as though I was wet-packed in a hydropathic establishment; but before I did that, I took off my shirt, gave one end to Jack Reynolds, and then wrung the superfluous and unusual water out of it. For a certain quantity always remained. Then I hung it up, and when one of the watch on deck came and roused us with, "Starbowlines ahoy! turn out, you sleepers!" the wet shirt had to be donned once more, then a wet jacket, and perhaps damp and dripping oilskins too. Yet I never suffered from rheumatism, nor did I have even a cold until I reached England and slept in comfort.

During this spell of bad weather we were served out no fresh water for washing purposes, and though we rinsed our faces every now and again with salt, we became darker and darker in complexion, until I, whose skin had been burnt to mahogany by more than two years of Australian bush life, began to look somewhat darker than a dirty mulatto. Yet as this melasma grew on us together, there were no remarks made until we ran out of the storms into fine warm weather, and were allowed some water to wash ourselves with. Then it was astonishing to see the difference that the fresh element and soap made upon us, and as we laughed in each other's clean faces, I considered that I had a complexion of almost feminine purity. Doubtless three weeks' unremoved grime made me fairer, just as the Alaskan Indian belles use soot and grease before a dance or festival, in order to make themselves whiter and, as they believe, more attractive.

It was a pleasant change to be able to go about one's work clothed only in a pair of "dungaree pants" and a "dungaree jumper," with the soft air blowing, and a bright sun overhead which would soon grow tropically hot. The only drawback to the weather was our energetic mate, who kept us hard at it with *souji-mouji* (strong alkali), paint and tar. We tarred down, rattled down (that is, put new ratlines on the rigging), painted the lower masts, yards, and rail, and I, who somehow showed a dexterity with the brush wholly surprising to myself, was set with one or two others to do the fine work in the cabin. I was even asked whether I had served my time as a painter. I did not give a direct answer, but allowed my questioner to believe that I had, for dexterity in a trade might always help me if I were bowled out in matters of seamanship, though I had almost ceased to fear that by this time, for when the painting was in progress we had run into the tropics, and the greater part of the passage was done.

It was in these latitudes and this vessel that I first noticed what I have never heard commented on or even mentioned. As I lay on my blankets on the top of the deckhouse, where I often made my bed, I used to stare dreamily straight up into the sky, past the royals and the spar yet above them, at the stars and moon floating in the deep serenity of space, and I often saw, by a curious transference of unperceived bodily motion, the whole heavens break loose, as it were, from their ancient holdings, and swing to and fro a few degrees on this and that side of the apparently stationary mast. I knew of course that the vessel itself was rolling, though so slightly that I could not perceive it save from the lofty spar which fulfilled the same office as the long index of a chemical balance which has to deal with weights inappreciable in an ordinary machine; but, nevertheless, it was hard to come to that conclusion, for the swing and rhythm of the passing and returning stars seemed so real and obvious. For I saw it, and felt that I was being conjured with by nature and the fallible senses. Yet it was a strangely beautiful illusion to see, though by surprise, the everlasting firmament, the very ether, play such fantastic tricks, for if they moved, what was stable, fixed, or eternal? As I wondered, perhaps there came a little larger swell from the west; the pointer moved a degree too far, the illusion was dissipated, the vessel itself was once more in motion that restored her to me as something almost alive and breathing, being no longer the sole fixed point beneath the loosed moon and stars.

The pleasantest hours of the whole passage were those spent working quietly up aloft with Jack Reynolds, when there was nothing very particular to be done down below, for we could sit near each other, spin short yarns, and chew tobacco *ad libitum*, provided we were careful to spit overboard. Our work at such times consisted in looking after all the innumerable trifles up aloft which require to be carefully attended to, and if at last we could find nothing that really wanted renewing, out came my knife from its sheath, a seizing disappeared overboard, and we put a new one in its place. "Just as well to be careful," Jack would say, grinning; "our lives might depend on it some day." For we would never willingly confess that we had nothing to do on the foremast lest the bo'son might find us some less pleasing task, such as his tribe have a knack of doing. Ours was a very good fellow, though, in his way and never surly with me, although he soon found out that I was not an able seaman of very long standing. Yet my unexpected dexterity in being able to make a complicated knot called a "Matthew Walker" on a four-stranded rope which a much older man had got confused about, impressed him very favourably, although from my not being able to do much simpler things, he looked on me as a queer mixture of cleverness and crass stupidity. But he was down on one man from Gravesend, who, though a fine fellow to look at and very good-natured, was extraordinarily dense, and had a rooted objection to going aloft any more than he could avoid. As he let this be seen, the bo'son invariably picked him out for any job which took him there, especially if it was such a thing as putting in the gilt trucks at the top of the masts, or fixing a dog-vane there. But Phil was very amusing to us, and had a standing grievance and topic of conversation. This is how it came about.

As is well known, it is customary on the 180th parallel of longitude to add a day to the reckoning when going east, and to subtract it going west. It thus fell out that we had two Fridays running, and it was a sore puzzle to poor Phil. We took it in turns to try to demonstrate it to him, but it was no use. His answer was to scratch his head and say, "I shall ask the pilot when he comes on board, and just you see, we shall be a day out in our reckoning. It's all foolishness; there never were two Fridays in any week. Why, man alive, there would be eight days in it, and that can't be, for the Bible says, 'Six days shalt thou labour and do all thou hast to do,' and here we've been working seven and you say it isn't Sunday till to-morrow. Why, you're all mad!" And away went Phil to meditate over it all his spare time, for every now and again he came to us with a fresh argument which he considered ought to settle the matter. When he did find out that somehow or other we were right, his confusion of mind was perfectly ludicrous.

By this time I was thoroughly at home with the ship and men, and I really liked the life. Though nothing earthly could induce me to go back to it, that four months' passage home before the mast always remains, in spite of its toil and hardship, as the happiest time in my life. I was absolutely healthy and as strong as a young bull; I could race up to the royal yard and down again without losing my wind, or even breathing hard; I could go hand-over-hand sixty feet up a rope, and when I lay down I went so fast asleep, that sometimes all the watch bellowed at me in vain, and had to shake me at last. And, best of all, I never thought for five consecutive seconds, and if I knew the deadly words "introspection" and "analysis," I never went through any such process as they imply. I might well be content to sing in the second dogwatch with the heartiest good-will, or to take a good-humoured rough-and-tumble over the hatch, until one of us got his head banged against a ringbolt or the spare-anchor stock, without losing my temper. As long as one is well and does not think of the future, such a life is really very happy, if the officers do not make their vessel a "hell afloat," as they too often do.

About two degrees to the north of the line we had a day or two of "doldrums," or calm weather, but the old *Wessex* managed for the greater part of the time to keep way on her, and slip along at a knot or even more, while half-a-dozen vessels were in sight from the main royal yard with their heads all round the compass. In this weather I almost prayed for a gale, for the chief officer began again to get so exacting with his *souji-mouji*, paint and tar, that we had no excuse for taking a handful of spun-yarn and a little tobacco aloft to wile away the time as we looked at the blue expanse of sea. I was glad when we ran out of the trades at last and got a gale off the Western Islands (the Azores), for "Hands shorten sail" only kept us busy for a time, and we could sit in idleness afterwards. Yet it blew hard with occasional tremendous squalls, which made everything crack again. We had shortened her down to the reefed foresail and close-reefed topsails, but it blew harder and harder, and when our watch turned out at midnight we found a heavy sea running, while the wind was blowing great guns. The port watch had passed the long gaskets, with which the sail is made fast when it is furled, as preventer rovings, or additional fastenings, to the foresail, which had come away more than six inches from the yard; but there had been nothing else to do, for all the seizings, &c., that Jack and I had worked at in the fine weather did their duty in foul. After answering to our name at the poop in pitchy darkness, we went forward to the foc'sle again and sat smoking in silence, as we could barely hear ourselves speak for the roaring of the wind and the groaning of the timbers. At two bells, or one o'clock, the bos'on's mate came to us. He spoke, but at first I could not hear what he said, though I caught the word "foretop-men" which was quite enough to show that whatever had to be done fell to me and Jack Reynolds. After some shouting, I made out that the outer part of the upper foretopsail had blown loose from its lashings and that we were to make it fast again. I called Jack, and we went up aloft in such darkness that I could not see my mate when he was two yards away. Now, as sailors know, when the upper topsail is lowered down on the lifts, and the lifts of the lower yard are hauled taut, the foot-rope of the higher yard is jammed so far underneath it as to be of less than no use at all for standing and working on. So when I saw that any attempt to touch the gasket would result in the whole yardarm getting adrift, I roared to Jack to go down and get some pieces of sinnet, or the plaited stuff of which gaskets are made, which I knew were in the foretop, and then clambered out to the lift, and by its aid got over the upper and stood on the lower yard, in order to be able to go to work when Jack returned. But by the time he had got into the foretop I heard a strange noise, half hiss, half roar, and looking up, and aft, I beheld a squall coming up astern that was seemingly a solid white wall of sea-mist, foam, and cloud.

I threw my arms round the lift, grasping my coat and arms on each side, and held on. When the squall struck us, the vessel groaned and shivered all over, and seemed to double her speed. I didn't think, indeed I could not, for the roar of the wind and hiss of the beaten seas were too deafening, too overwhelming;  but I felt as if the masts must go over the side, that in the nature of things they ought to, for no work of man could be capable of resisting such tremendous power. And I clung on with desperation. Had I been on the weather-side of the yard I should have been in safety, so long as the masts stood; but as it was, the wind blew me away from it, once lifting my feet off the yard below, trying to tear asunder my gripped hands and locked arms with a force that seemed physical, intelligent, and alive, while the level spray struck me, blind and smarting, like stinging hail. It was a wonder that the sail, of which a small part was already loose, did not break its lashings and strike me off the yard like a thread of rejected spun yarn, and had not the gaskets been new on the foremast, this most assuredly would have happened. I cannot tell how long this squall lasted, I think it was nearly ten minutes; but if I am ever asked, I can say the longest ten minutes I ever knew were spent up aloft off the Western Islands. When the worst blew over, Jack came up with a bundle of sinnet and a grin on his round face, asking, " How did you like that, old man?" I passed the new lashing round the bellying sail, and we went down, very contented to descend leisurely, and not in a hurry together with the topmasts.

From that time forward we had no more bad weather, and we ran for the English Channel with a good westerly breeze until we were in soundings (seventy fathoms, sand and shells), when the wind changed to the east, dead in our teeth, and we had to beat to windward in short tacks. There is nothing more exasperating to a sailor than to have to do this on his homeward run. He is so eager to get ashore, so full of earnestness in desiring to put to the proof his resolution that "this time" he will not get drunk as usual, that his new virtue finds the delay of temptation too hard to be borne.

There were many such among my shipmates, and though I laughed then, I think now that there was more of pathos than comedy in those resolutions which were so soon to be broken.

But beating up Channel gave me no time for moralizing, and the chief officer was far too intent on having everything as fresh as a daisy to leave us in idleness for a moment. From " Hands 'bout ship " to the paint-pots and holystones was the perpetual change, and when we picked up a tug off the Wight and made the sails fast for the last time, it was only to leave us more time for scrubbing paint and cleaning brasswork.

But how glad I was to greet England once more! Even the long wake of the lights of the Lizard made me feel at home again, and when I saw the coast half covered with cloud, I could have shouted with a joy that none who stay at home can comprehend. But there was one thing that struck me in England as very strange, not to say painful, and that was the vivid colour of the pastures. We are quite proud of our perpetual verdure ; but, to tell the truth, the tint of the grass after the soberer dull greys and greens and browns of Australia was extremely unpleasant to my eye. I thought the colour glaring, not to say inartistic ; it certainly was not unnatural, and yet it struck me as being as nearly that as if some one had deliberately painted the fields. It took me months to get reconciled to it.

After the long passage of 104 days, I had some

right to think that I should not be called upon to do anything that I did not have sufficient knowledge of to carry through, but I was nearly reckoning without my host. Our "mud pilot," as sailors call the pilots of inland waters, whom we had picked up at the entrance of London River, sent men into the chains to heave the lead, and one of our crew, a half-bred Yankee, who was otherwise a good seaman, declined to go, as he, in spite of fifteen years at sea, had never done such work before. The second mate accepted his excuse, much to old Jack Shaw's disgust, for it was his next turn. He likewise refused to do that duty, and his refusal brought the officer into the foc'sle to see what this unexpected insubordination meant.

"Shaw, go in the chains," he said shortly.

"Can't heave the lead," answered old Jack sullenly, though every one knew he could. "Why should I be able to do it, when this Yankee able-seaman can't?"

"No more jaw," said the officer; and Jack, who saw he was not to be trifled with, went out grumbling.

Then Mr. Jackson asked us all in turn whether we could heave the lead. Receiving affirmative answers, he came to me.

"Mitchell, can you?" said he.

Now I knew the "marks" and "deeps" of the hand line, but had never seen it heaved, as far as I remembered. Nevertheless I would tackle it, or anything else, rather than say I could not.

"I guess so," I answered.

"What do you mean by 'I guess so'?" he asked, rather angrily.

"Well, then, I can, sir," I answered in desperation, wondering very much if I could all the time.

I was in a fix, but I determined to carry it through, so I went on deck and watched old Shaw at work, until I perceived that it was not so hard as I had imagined. In another hour I was in the chains myself, singing out, "By the mark, seven," "Quarter, less eight," "By the deep, nine," as bold as brass, until a sudden fog compelled us to anchor. When the "mud-hook" was on the ground, and things made snug, I went into the foc'sle to find the Yankee in low spirits, and old Shaw still grumbling against him. "What kind of a sailor did he call himself, when even a young chap like Mitchell could go in the chains and do his duty?" That was what old Shaw wanted to know.

I chuckled and turned away, and nobody, not even Jack Reynolds, knew that it was my first experience of heaving the lead.

In the morning we hove the anchor up to the most beautiful chanty that sailors sing, "Homeward bound," and by ten o'clock we entered the south-west dock. I was the first on shore with a warp to help to make her fast, and I shall never forget the sensation of feeling the gravel grinding under my heels when I sprang from the vessel's side. When the ship is alongside the wharf and secured, the crew are free, and in a few minutes we tumbled down below, shifted our working clothes and donned our best, which in my case I am bound to say were nothing to boast of. Indeed I had a discussion with Reynolds as to whether I was well enough dressed to go home, for I had in nearly three years of rough life almost lost the notion of dress. Finally, in deference to Jack's opinion, I consented to go to the Sailors' Home in Well Street, until we were paid off, by which time I could get a new rig-out. A van from the Home was waiting for those of us who wished to go there, and as I rode off in it I passed Shaw, whose wife had come to meet him. I called his attention to my coach-and-six, and he chuckled a grim farewell to "Lord Paget," as he still nicknamed me.

When we reached the Home, there was a crowd of the lowest men and women in East London waiting outside, and they almost stormed the van trying to persuade us from entering it. When the big door opened and we drove in, a wild and savage yell of rage and disappointment rose from the shut-out mob at losing what might be their last chance of getting hold of men with money. For once in the Home, there is much in favour of staying there, and Jack is too busy amusing himself to shift his "dunnage," as he calls his impedimenta, after he has once deposited it in safe keeping.

As for me, I remained there three days, saw some aspects of life which were new to me, and then, just for a change, I went to stay in the West of London.

July, 1891.

THE END.

www.ingramcontent.com/pod-product-compliance
Lightning Source LLC
Chambersburg PA
CBHW032135230426
43672CB00011B/2343